CONSECRATIONS,

BLESSINGS

AND

PRAYERS

CONSECRATIONS
BLESSINGS
✝
PRAYERS

A PASTORAL COMPANION TO THE RITUAL
AND TO THE BOOK OF BLESSINGS

CANTERBURY
PRESS
Norwich

© in this compilation Sean Finnegan 2018

First published in 2005 by
The Canterbury Press Norwich
(a publishing imprint of Hymns Ancient & Modern Limited,
a registered charity)
St Mary's Works, St Mary's Plain
Norwich, Norfolk NR3 3BH

Second Edition 2018

British Library Cataloguing in Publication Data

A catalogue record for this book is available
from the British Library

ISBN 978 1 78622 085 1

Printed in Great Britain by
CPI Group (UK) Ltd

CONTENTS

INTRODUCTION

All you works of the Lord, O bless the Lord,
To him be highest glory and praise for ever !

Dan 3:52

THE title of this little book reveals succinctly the nature of its contents, as a good title should: consecrations, blessings and prayers. It may strike many would-be readers as unusual that such a collection should be offered to the public at large. There are many compilations of prayers available; the compiler of this volume has himself already published one such. Blessings and consecrations, on the other hand, will seem to many to belong to a category of prayer which is more solemn, even arcane—a matter for professional clergy perhaps, for whom there already exist the official liturgical books. The purpose of this book is to make available to the general reader prayers and blessings which are suitable for use in private, to sustain personal prayer and meditation, to offer texts suitable for use in various circumstances of daily life. I believe that it will thus be of great utility to the laity, precisely because it offers texts capable of being prayed in a very wide variety of circumstances. It will doubtless attract most attention from Catholics, since indeed the majority of the texts it contains are from our own tradition. Nevertheless, it may be hoped that many Christians from other traditions will find it useful. Many non-Catholics may discover here the real meaning of rites and ceremonies which they may hitherto have considered suspect, or even downright superstitious. Whatever one's attitude towards blessings and consecrations, most I think will agree that the selections of scripture texts and prayers for various occasions, private and public, are useful and apposite to the business of leading one's life under God's guidance and offering to him our efforts and our cares.

The variety of circumstances for which this book is able to make suggestions will also, I think, render it useful to many clergy. It may indeed serve to supplement the official books currently in use by offering texts which either come from other, older traditions, or which are adapted to circumstances and uses not foreseen by the liturgical books themselves. I myself, as a parish priest in a rural environment, have more than once had occasion to regret that neither the present Book of Blessings nor the old Roman Ritual seems to have anything to offer which is wholly suited to this or that occasion. It is beyond the limits of human frailty (or indeed of available space!) to provide texts suitable for every conceivable need, precisely because the nature of a blessing is to offer a way of sanctifying ordinary human existence, marked as this is by an infinite variety. Fr Finnegan's offering is thus not intended to be exhaustive, still less to supplant or compete with the liturgical books themselves, but even a cursory perusal of it has already suggested to me that it will be a welcome resource for parish life.

In saying that the nature of a blessing involves the sanctifying of human existence, I am of course begging the question for which this modest introduction aspires to provide an answer: what are blessings and consecrations? In what way are they able to contribute to the spiritual life of the ordinary Christian, to support and further his or her personal prayer? The phenomenon of blessing is well known to anthropologists and sociologists of religion. Its long history predates the emergence of Judaeo-Christian revealed religion by many millennia. The Latin word *benedicere,* which we translate by the word 'bless', is itself a perfect homonym of the Greek *eulogein.* These terms mean literally 'to speak well', at first in the sense of the art of correct speech, but quickly they acquire a technical sense which derives from the notion of speaking well of or for someone, the opposite of speaking ill of them. To bless is thus to praise or extol someone, and we find an example of this in the Gloria of the Mass: we praise you, we bless you, we adore you, we glorify you, we give you thanks for your great glory ...

In the Greek version of the Bible, the Septuagint, where it is used to translate the Hebrew *barak,* the verb 'to bless' takes on a new meaning. Whereas the original notion had an 'upward' meaning, of praise directed from humanity to God or the gods, the term now comes to represent a 'downward' motion, whereby the verb takes on the sense of a saving force which comes from God who blesses his people, and bestows on them the blessings of his grace. The noun *berakah* (plural *berakoth*) derived from it, comes to signify at one and the same time the act of divine giving, God's saving action, and the gifts he bestows: life, health, freedom from servitude, strength against the enemies of his people and so on. The 'upwards' meaning is not abolished by this change (as we see in the famous verse from Daniel quoted above) and the life of the pious

Jew is led to the rhythm of the daily *berakoth*. These are the daily prayers of praise which Christ himself would have known and used, accompanying every meaningful gesture of daily life, and most significantly meals, when God is acknowledged as source of life and sustenance. The Paschal meal was of course the most notable of these 'blessings', where the thanksgiving is directed to the God who saved his people from slavery in Egypt, and our Lord himself gave a new meaning to these rites[1] when, having said the *berakoth* over the bread and the cup, he gave to the Church his people the saving mysteries of his body and blood, thus uniting in a single act the 'upward' and 'downward' meanings of the verb. The Eucharist is thus the supreme 'blessing': the perfect sacrifice of praise to the Father, and the transmission in return of his most perfect gift to his Church, that of his only Son.

At the same time as this new 'downward' meaning of blessing comes to complement the first, 'upward' one, we see human beings act as God's intermediary in bestowing his blessings. We might recall how important to Jacob was the blessing of his father Isaac, so vital in fact that he was willing, with his mother's connivance, to defraud his brother Esau in order to obtain it! (Gen 27:27–29). The Book of Numbers (6:23–27) transmits to us a blessing which is put into the mouth of Aaron, and which was doubtless already, when it was committed to writing, a liturgical formula, as it is even today:

The Lord bless you and keep you. The Lord make his countenance to shine upon you, and be gracious to you. The Lord turn his face to you and give you his peace!

Just as people become in this way 'ministers' of God's blessings, so ritual gestures come to accompany them—most notably the 'laying on of hands'. This action, meant to confirm the words of the prayer of blessing and to 'lay hold' of its beneficiary on God's behalf, will become in the Christian liturgy the sacramental gesture par excellence. It is retained in baptism, ordinations, confirmation, confession, the anointing of the sick, and in the Eucharist where it is performed on the bread and wine about to be consecrated. In these rites it is usually complemented by the sign of the cross, which seems to be a natural extension of the laying on of hands. It accompanies that pre-Christian gesture as a way of reminding us that for Christians all God's supernatural gifts come from the cross of Christ. In the non-sacramental blessings, it fulfils this same function.

Christ in the Gospels, as we have seen, takes to himself these religious practices of his people. Besides the supreme example of the Last Supper to which I have already referred, we see him blessing children and laying hands on them (Mk 10:16), and lifting his hands to bless his disciples as he ascends to his Father (Lk 24:50–51). We see him also blessing his Father in the 'upward' movement of praise: 'I bless you, Father, Lord of heaven and earth ...' (Lk 10:21).

Small wonder then that the Christian Church from its origins should have taken over the Jewish practice of blessings as a manner of sanctifying daily life and celebrating God's gifts. As the Church became separate from the synagogue, paradoxically she became less diffident about taking over elements from Jewish worship: incense, chants, Old Testament symbolism, even the very word 'priest' which replaced little by little the primitive 'presbyter' or 'elder'. The same development is conspicuous in the use of blessings. In the Apostolic Tradition dating from the turn of the second and third centuries we find blessings concerning oil, wine, cheese, milk, honey and other fruits of the earth, as well as for the light. These are blessings of the 'upward' type, praising God for his gifts:

> for everything we receive we should give thanks to God the Holy One, receiving it in this way for his glory. [2]

But as time goes on we find that benedictions of the 'downward' type predominate more and more, asking God's blessings on human life and work.

This should not surprise us; nor should we see these two functions as in conflict. Rather their complementary nature is shown by the fact that we find quotations from early Fathers where both senses of the notion of 'blessing' are found. We find St Gregory the Great enjoining on his flock the fast of the September Ember Days (a sort of harvest fast, as opposed to a harvest festival) saying

> It is great in the sight of the Lord ... and most precious to him, when God is glorified in the works of his servants, and the author of all goodness is blessed with much thanksgiving.[3]

But we find also, much earlier than this, St Basil telling us that 'a blessing is the communication of sanctification,' [4] while in the West St Ambrose combines succinctly both aspects when he writes 'a blessing is the conferral of sanctification and the rendering of thanks.' [5]

These blessings concern first of all persons: bishops, priests, deacons, readers, virgins, widows, abbots and abbesses, penitents, catechumens, the sick and dying, pregnant women, children, &c. But we also find blessings for objects; first of all those concerning Christian worship (church buildings, sacred vessels, baptismal fonts, crosses, oil, wax, water, salt, incense, &c.) but then also those concerned with everyday life: (seeds for planting, harvests, the earth, first fruits, animals, houses, wells, clothes &c.). The first category of blessings are considered as taking the persons and objects out of the realm of the profane and dedicating them to God's service, to the point where continued profane usage of them would be sacrilege. They will tend to become known as 'consecrations' and be reserved to ministers endowed with special authority, chiefly bishops. The second category does not remove the blessed person or object from ordinary life but intends to impart God's favour to the pursuance of their natural function. They too will tend to be reserved more and more to priests, although in some cases deacons and clerics in minor orders would continue to perform them.

The practice of such benedictions became common first in monasteries and spread throughout society, where they became an integral part of Christian life and devotion. By the eighth and ninth centuries, their number was legion. One scholar has published a collection of more than two thousand! [6] After the Council of Trent an effort was made to restrict their number. The *Rituale Romanum* of 1614 contained eleven blessings reserved to the bishop, and only eight to be used by simple priests. But this early effort at rationalization did not stand the test of time, for diocesan books, doubtless under pressure from pastors constrained to offer their flocks a richer fare, were continually adding others, and Rome herself eventually followed suit in the nineteenth century. By 1925 there were 150 blessings in the Roman Ritual. Several of them are contained, in an English translation, in this book.

The *Liber Benedictionum* published by Rome in 1984 followed a similar trajectory. At first it was intended to give a detailed presentation of the theology of blessings, followed by thirty formulas for diverse specific needs. It was thought that vernacular versions elaborated by local hierarchies would complete these with others adapted to specific local needs. This initial project was to be modified in the ten years which intervened between its being officially proposed and its final publication in 1984, by when more than eighty formulas had been included. Small wonder then that almost immediately complaints began to be heard about the gaps in its range of propositions. [7] This book might be considered at least in part then as a reflection of the need ever felt by the faithful and their pastors for a wide variety of blessings suited to the diversities of everyday life.

What meaning then should we assign to the practice of blessing persons and objects, in the light of the biblical and historical material by means of which I have attempted to illustrate this meaning? We could do worse than to quote from the monumental *Dictionnaire d'Archéologie Chrétienne et de Liturgie,* where the eminent Fr Baudot wrote in 1925 that a blessing is

> an action accomplished by a man whom the Church has invested with a divine power with the aim of calling down by prayer, divine favour upon persons or things. [8]

However, we should notice how this definition is incomplete, for it only takes into account what we have called the 'downward' motion of invoking God's aid, and neglects to mention the 'upward' motion of praise directed to God for his good gifts.

The new liturgical *Book of Blessings* remedies this oversight very well. The Second Vatican Council had led the way by seeking to return to the most authentic traditions in every aspect of Catholic life. With regard to the sacramentals, the category to which blessings belong, the Council lays out the character of the reforms which are to be made:

> With the passage of time, however, there have crept into the rites of the sacraments and sacramentals certain features which have rendered their nature and purpose far from clear to the people of today; hence some changes have become necessary to adapt them to the needs of our own times. [9]

In accordance with these principles, the *Book of Blessings* sets out to restore the imbalance caused when the 'doxological', or 'upward' content of the notion of blessing was squeezed out by too unilateral an emphasis on the sanctification of people and objects. All the blessings contained in it contain an 'upward' motion of praise as well as a plea for a 'downward' bestowal of God's grace. We might speak, in a way which mirrors the structure of the Eucharistic Liturgy, that blessing *par excellence,* of an element of *anamnesis,* the calling to mind of God's marvellous deeds for his people, and an element of *epiclesis,* the calling down of God's blessings on that same people. In addition, the new Ritual for blessings invariably offers a selection of scripture texts as a prelude and an inspiration for the anamnetic element in the prayers which follow. Fr Finnegan's selection follows the official ritual in these respects, and allows for this element of praise and even instruction by providing scripture texts and psalms and prayers to complement the central prayers of blessings.

In one respect however Fr Finnegan does not follow the new ritual. The *Liber Benedictionum,* in its zeal to combat the excesses of former times, when certain forms of popular piety doubtless were wont to emphasize sacred objects at the expense of holy living, ruthlessly chooses to exclude the idea of the sanctification of matter from its purview. Even when it provides blessings for objects, it asks almost exclusively for God's blessing on their users, and not for the sanctification of the objects themselves. At a time when ecumenism has helped us rediscover the worship of the Christian East, with its strong sense of Christ's saving work embracing the whole cosmos, and when people everywhere are waking up to the vital need to respect the environment, this desacralisation of the material world seems to many a regrettable concession to the Enlightenment's 'disenchanting' of the natural universe. There has been much criticism of this aspect of the *Book of Blessings,* which was one of the last productions of the post-conciliar liturgical reform. Indeed, one cannot help but wonder if this rejection of something so natural to Catholic piety has not contributed to the lack of uptake from which the Book of Blessings has undoubtedly suffered. Many priests, if they continue to bless objects at all, use the prayers from the old Ritual, and as far as one can tell this has never been forbidden by any authority. By giving many of the older texts in a good and readily understood translation, Fr Finnegan has done more than offer perplexed clergy a resource from which they can cull texts they may judge more satisfying; he has given us all an opportunity to rediscover the sense of the material universe as included in Christ's redeeming work.

Let us leave the final word on this point to Dom Cipriano Vaggagini, one of the leading architects of the liturgical reform: 'Even in the simple blessings of infrahuman things,' he writes,

there is included the idea that God, always in consideration of the prayer of the Church, will grant, in accordance with the designs of his providence, a special protection to the object itself and to the use which man makes of it, with a view to permitting him the more easily to work out his salvation. It is noteworthy that in the formulas of these blessings there is not infrequently a sense of the cosmic unity of the Kingdom of God and a consciousness that even the infrahuman creation, in its own way, is called to co-operation therein.

Vaggagini goes on to enumerate the great realities of Christian doctrine which are exemplified and given expression in this way: the unity of the cosmos; the cosmic universality of the fall, as well as that of the redemption accomplished by Christ; 'man as microcosm and focal point of the universe'; and 'the sacred worth of sensible things as gifts of God to man, and as instruments of man in going to God'. He concludes:

all of this is opposed in the highest degree to pantheism, polytheism, magic, naturalism, and to every kind of secularism.

With this magnificent summing up of the value of blessings directed to objects, we have come close to being able to give a general outline of what I hoped to do at the start of this introduction: to give an account of what part blessings, consecrations and the other prayers contained in this book can play in helping today's Christians to grow as praying members of God's people. For the Catholic there exist a special category of blessings, which are normally carried out by persons deputed to do so by the Church; when this happens they are called sacramentals, that is, rites which in some way are analogous to the seven sacraments which Christ gave to his Church. They are unlike the sacraments in that they do not cause a growth in holiness by the mere fact of carrying out the rite itself, while the sacraments do because it is Christ himself who acts directly through the actions of his minister. [10] They do so because of, and in proportion to, the desire of the one who performs the blessing, and of those who ask for it to be performed. [11] Because of this, they are not magical gestures, but simply ways of praying. Insofar as they are done using formulas approved by the Church and carried out be her ministers, for Catholics they are prayers which have a special place and efficacy among those which fill our Christian lives with the presence of God. Let us read what Vatican II has to say on the subject:

Holy Mother Church has, moreover, instituted sacramentals. These are sacred signs which bear a resemblance to the sacraments: they signify effects, particularly of a spiritual kind, which are obtained through the Church's intercession. By them men are disposed to receive the chief effect of the sacraments, and various occasions in life are rendered holy.

Thus, for well-disposed members of the faithful, the liturgy of the sacraments and sacramentals sanctifies almost every event in their lives; they are given access to the stream of divine grace which flows from the paschal mystery of the passion, death, and resurrection of Christ, the font from which all sacraments and sacramentals draw their power. There is hardly any proper use of material things which cannot thus be directed toward the sanctification of men and the praise of God. [12]

One application of the Council's reformist principles made by the new *Book of Blessings* was to relax somewhat the rules of the old Ritual concerning the ministers empowered to impart blessings. The more solemn blessings or consecrations of liturgical objects—vestments, chalices and patens for example—are no longer reserved to the Bishop but may be carried out by any priest. Deacons may now carry out most blessings, and some may be performed by those instituted in the new, non-clericalized ministries of lector, acolyte, and catechist (although in all these cases only in the absence of a priest). Heads of families may bless their children. In all these cases blessings thus performed will be truly sacramentals, if done according to approved rites and with the intention to gain the graces and benefits for which the prayers ask. This widening of the category of sacramentals, making them available where a priest is not easily to be had, is most surely to be welcomed. It may be supposed that these conditions also apply when, for a just reason, the minister has recourse to a blessing taken from a formerly approved source. *Favorabilia sunt multiplicanda*—good things should be given liberally—was the wise maxim of the canonists of old.

What of the Christian layperson, perhaps not even a Catholic, who would like to put this book to its fullest use and derive the fullest benefit from it? Of course, here is nothing to stop anyone taking even the liturgical prayers gathered here and adapting them to non-liturgical use, as prayers of thanksgiving for a particular gift or petition for a given need. Above all, it is here in particular that we may appreciate the large selection of prayers for occasions many and various, which complement the blessings because, like them, they are designed to recognize and to request the presence of God, and the abundance of his gifts, in the manifold circumstances of everyday life. In Church, as in the home, sometimes indeed on public occasions, the ordinary Christian will find texts and prayers capable of sustaining and inspiring prayer. Fr Finnegan has gathered together texts from many sources, sometimes translating, sometimes composing them himself, but always with clarity of style and lightness of touch. Occasionally there are welcome touches of humour—I particularly like the prayer for a meeting 'likely to be stormy' and wish I had had it to hand on some occasions in the past!

All in all, the book will have served us well if it helps us to recognise the twofold manner in which our lives as Christians should be full of 'blessings'. First we should ever be lifting up our hearts in praise and thanks to God who has given us so many blessings in creating and redeeming us. Secondly we all need to ask him constantly to pour down upon us the blessings we need, both spiritual and temporal, in order to continue our journey towards him sustained and refreshed. We should always bear in mind that the efficacy of our prayers will depend infinitely more on the sincerity of dispositions of faith, hope and love than on finding the right words to express them. Still, the Catholic will have a special affection for the prayers we receive from the Church and which we pray in union of heart and voice with her. And above all, we should remember that both senses of 'blessing' are most truly realized in the highest Christian prayer, the Eucharistic Sacrifice, in which we bless God through, with and in our Lord Jesus Christ, and receive in return that Christ who is our most precious blessing. The Mass, Vatican II reiterated, is the 'source and summit' of the Church's life. Let it be for each one of us the summit towards which we lift our hands and voices in praise of God, and the source at which we drink with joy the infinite blessings of his grace.

Mark Drew

March 2018

NOTES

1. In writing this I am prescinding from the question so hotly debated among New Testament scholars as to whether or not the Last Supper actually was a Passover Meal.

2. Ap.Trad. 32.

3. Cf *Sources Chrétiennes* n° 200, Léo le Grand, Sermons, vol IV, p. 94, Paris 1973.

4. Letter 199 to Amphilochius, PG32, 723D, see Loeb edition vol. III p. 119.

5. *Benedictio (est) sanctificationis et gratiarum votiva collatio.* De Benedictionibus Patriarcharum, ch. 22, PL 14, 676A.

6. E. Moeller *Corpus Benedictionum Pontificalium,* Corpus Christianorum Latinum, nos 162, 162 1,B and C, 1973–1979.

7. An interesting example is the article published by the influential French liturgist Pierre Jounel in *La Maison Dieu* (175, 1988, p. 47) where he complains of the lack of blessings covering civic life. The astute reader will note that this shortcoming is made good in the present volume !

8. Article *Bénédictions* in DACL vol. II/I, col. 671.

9. Ibid, 62.

10. This is the meaning of the scholastic term *ex opere operato,* describing how the sacraments operate through their own inherent power.

11. *Ex opere operantis (ecclesiæ).*

12. Decree *Sacrosanctum Concilium,* on the Sacred Liturgy, nos 60, 61.

COMPILER'S INTRODUCTION

THE idea for this book arose from the difficulty that I, the compiler, a priest, have experienced in concrete pastoral situations when trying to confine myself to the use of the official books designed to assist me in the occasional rites at which a pastor is required from time to time to officiate. Often their writers seem never actually to have experienced the situations in which their compositions are supposed to be used. For instance, the scriptural readings and intercessions suggested by the Book of Blessings when blessing a rosary seem unnecessarily elaborate, whereas the rite for blessing a house in the old Ritual (which, as Fr Drew writes in his introduction, many clergy still use, decades after its supposed supplantation) seems almost indecently brief. The *Veritas Book of Blessing Prayers* is to be commended as one serious attempt to address this pastoral lacuna; this book aspires to be another.

I should state from the outset, then, that this book is designed to be *useable*. Since the content in no way pretends either to be or to replace the official prayer of the Church, but simply function as a pastoral assistant to that prayer, the user should make any and every adaptation that seems to be called for in the situation that confronts him or her. These are not official rites that have to be observed in their integrity.

Most, if not all, priests in their grant of faculties on ordination are given the authority to bless anything with a simple sign of the cross. This book simply supplies prayers to accompany this blessing. Sometimes these are translated anew from old sources, at other times entirely new prayers have been composed. Other material, except where noted in the text, is believed to be in the public forum; if there has been any unintentional use of copyright material, the compiler offers his apologies and will of course make all corrections in any subsequent editions.

When blessings are given by a priest in a more formal setting, it is customary to wear cassock and cotta (surplice) or an alb, with a stole (usually white, unless the blessing has a penitential character, when purple is used). It is also usual to sprinkle holy water when the blessing has been completed, but this can be left to the discretion of the user.

The response *And with your spirit* to the various greetings in this book is now familiar to Catholics. Others may of course choose *And also with you* instead. The translation of the scriptures used in this volume is the compiler's own gentle updating of the Douai-Rheims version, chosen in order to combine a certain *gravitas* with necessary clarity.

I am most grateful to all those who have assisted me in the production of this book, especially Fr Dominic Jacob for much good advice, Fr Mark Drew who has written the splendid theological introduction, also the Reverend William Perry, and many many others to whom I owe so much. This expanded second edition owes much to the Reverend Christine Smith and her friends for coming up with ideas for circumstances when a blessing or prayer might be useful. Christine is also the publisher and has been supportive and kind over many years.

S.A.F.

Sexagesima, 2018

CONSECRATIONS,

BLESSINGS

AND

PRAYERS

A SERVICE OF BLESSING

There may be occasions when a simple blessing is not enough, and the pastor may wish to add solemnity to the blessing he or she is adminstering. In this case, the blessing may be expanded into a short service along these lines.

In the name of the Father, and of the Son, ✠ and of the Holy Spirit. Amen.

℣. The Lord be with you.
℟. **And with your spirit.**

Let us pray.

GRACIOUS God, whose Son has enlightened us with the grace of the Gospel and brought us salvation, send your Holy Spirit on us today, that all we do and say may be inspired by you, the source of all holiness and grace. May what we bless be blessed by you, and made another channel of your goodness towards us who are so undeserving of your love. Through our Lord Jesus Christ your Son, who lives and reigns with you in the unity of the Holy Spirit, one God for ever and ever. Amen.

READING

HOMILY, IF DESIRED

BLESSING PRAYER

OUR FATHER

℣. The Lord be with you.
℟. **And with your spirit.**

May Almighty God bless you, the Father, the Son ✠ and the Holy Spirit. Amen.

℣. Let us bless the Lord.
℟. **Thanks be to God.**

PART I

CONSECRATIONS

Those things which, by their nature, are permanently set apart—consecrated for ever to the Lord—in such a way that they should never be used for secular purposes.

BELLS

The Solemn Blessing
or 'Baptism' of Bells

THE ANCIENT AND LONGER FORM

The bell should be suspended in the church from a frame in such a way that it may be touched and rung, and placed so that it may easily be gone around. Before the blessing begins, some or all of the following psalms may be sung:

> Psalm 53 (54), Lord save me according to your name.
> Psalm 56 (57), Have mercy on me God, have mercy.
> Psalm 66 (67), May God have mercy on us and bless us.
> Psalm 69 (70), O God come to my assistance.
> Psalm 85 (86), Bow down your ear O Lord and hear me.
> Psalm 129 (130), Out of the depths I cry to you O Lord.

℣. Lord, have mercy.
℟. **Lord, have mercy.**

℣. Christ, have mercy.
℟. **Christ, have mercy.**

℣. Lord, have mercy.
℟. **Lord, have mercy.**

Our Father.

℣. Blessed be the name of the Lord.
℟. **Both now and evermore.**

℣. O Lord, hear my prayer.
℟. **And let my cry come to you.**

℣. The Lord be with you.
℟. **And with your spirit.**

Let us pray.

ALMIGHTY God, who commanded by means of your servant and lawgiver Moses that silver trumpets be made for the priests to call the people together at the time of sacrifice, and to prepare them for worship, we ask that you send your Holy Spirit to bless ✠ this bell by our humble service, that by its ringing the people may be called to church, and thence to eternal life. And as its sweet sound swells in their ears, may your holy people grow in their devotion to the faith, may the traps of their enemy be destroyed; the shattering hailstones, the forceful tempests, the powerful thunder and lightning; may all these powers of the heavens be laid low by the strength of your right arm, and may our spiritual enemies tremble at its ringing and flee before the sign of the cross which we will make upon it. And may the same Lord, who suffered upon the cross and by its means swallowed up death, graciously grant our prayers, who lives and reigns with the Father and the Holy Spirit, one God for ever and ever. Amen.

Incense is placed in the thurible. Then the celebrant goes around the bell, sprinkling it with holy water. It is customary that the chant Asperges me *(You will sprinkle me with hyssop) be sung. Then, the celebrant circles the bell, censing it.*

Let us pray.

ALMIGHTY Lord, Jesus Christ, who calmed the storm on the Sea of Galilee, we pray that you send your Holy Spirit upon this bell, that the enemy may always flee from its ringing, that it may call the Christian people to worship, that it may terrify foreign invaders, and that it might comfort your people as the harp of David comforted his listeners. And when this bell is lifted up to ring among the clouds, may the hands of the angels reach down to protect this church and faithful people that they may be brought one day to salvation in mind and body; for you live and reign with the Father and the same Holy Spirit, one God for ever and ever. Amen.

The celebrant makes the sign of the cross on the bell, saying:

We name and bless ✠ this bell in honour of Saint N. Amen.

Everyone present may now sound the newly blessed bell.

Shorter Blessing of a Bell

A reading from the book of Psalms.   Ps. 150

P RAISE the Lord in his holy place:
  praise him in the firmament of his power.
Praise him for his mighty acts,
    praise him according to the excellence of his greatness.
Praise him with the sound of trumpet,
    praise him with psaltery and harp.
Praise him with timbrel and choir,
    praise him with strings and organs.
Praise him on well-sounding cymbals,
    praise him on cymbals of joy.
Let everything that breathes praise the Lord!

Let us pray.

B E with us now, Lord God, and hear us as we ask you to bless this
  bell which we consecrate to your glory. May we always be quick
  to hear your call, and be reminded to honour you in our hearts as
we hear it ring in our neighbourhood. May its voice be a daily remind-
er to us of your call to holiness and virtue so that, loving you and our
neighbour, we and all those who through the years ahead may listen
to this bell, be called finally to the joy of heaven. Through Christ our
Lord. Amen.

We name this bell N., and we bless it in the name of the Lord: Father,
Son ✠ and Holy Spirit. Amen.

THE CONSECRATION OF
SACRED VESTMENTS

℣. Our help is in the name of the Lord.
℟. **Who made heaven and earth.**
℣. The Lord be with you.
℟. **And with your spirit.**

Let us pray.

A LMIGHTY, eternal God, who commanded through Moses your servant that sacred vestments of high priests, priests and Levites should be consecrated for the proper performance of their ministry before you, and for the honour and glory of your name: come, we pray, at our call and refresh us with your grace; pour forth your blessing, that this vestment/these vestments may be sanctified ✠ and consecrated for your fit worship in the sacred mysteries; may Bishops, Priests and Deacons, thus vested, be protected from wandering thoughts, or temptations from the evil one, to the fitting and proper performance of your worship, and to their own perseverance in your service. Through Christ our Lord. Amen.

and/or

G OD, mighty conqueror, creator and sanctifier of all things, graciously hear our prayers that these vestments/this vestment for the use of bishops, priests or deacons in their sacred offices be blessed ✠, sanctified and consecrated with your grace, so that all who use them be fitted for your worship and serve you praiseworthily and faithfully. Through Christ our Lord. Amen.

and/or

L ORD God Almighty, who commanded Moses your servant to make vestments for priests and Levites to serve before the Ark of the Covenant, and filled him with the spirit of wisdom for this purpose, we pray that you bless ✠ and consecrate this vestment/

these vestments for the rites of your worship, and grant that those who wear them for service at your altar may be filled with the sevenfold gifts of your Spirit, being vested with charity, and with faith fruitful in good works to bring them to everlasting life. Through Christ our Lord. Amen.

THE CONSECRATION
OF ALTAR CLOTHS

℣. Our help is in the name of the Lord.
℟. Who made heaven and earth.
℣. The Lord be with you.
℟. And with your spirit.

Let us pray.

L ORD God Almighty, who during forty days commanded Moses your servant to make cloths and ornaments, and which Miriam wove and sewed that they might be used in the service of the Ark of the Covenant, bless ✠, we pray, these white garments with which we will clothe the altar, symbol of the cloths which wrapped the body of your only-begotten Son, and grant that our service may be as pure and unspotted as these cloths which we dedicate to your service. Through the same Christ our Lord. Amen.

and/or

L ORD, hear our prayers, and bless ✠ these cloths (this cloth) prepared for the service of your altar. Through Christ our Lord. Amen.

THE CONSECRATION OF VESSELS

℣. Our help is in the name of the Lord.
℞. **Who made heaven and earth.**
℣. The Lord be with you.
℞. **And with your spirit.**

Let us pray.

ALMIGHTY, ever-living God, who have made your faithful people receptacles of grace and temples of the Holy Spirit, hear us as we consecrate these vessels to your service, and grant that as we use them to your greater glory, you may be pleased with our worship and grant us those things we seek from your almighty goodness. Through Christ our Lord. Amen.

and/or

LORD, hear our prayers, and bless ✠ these vessels prepared for the service of your altar. Through Christ our Lord. Amen.

Holy water is sprinkled.

A PYX

ALMIGHTY, ever-living God, be pleased to bless ✠ this pyx, fashioned as a resting place for the Body of our Lord Jesus Christ your Son, and set it apart from any other use. Through the same Christ our Lord. Amen.

Holy water is sprinkled.

The Consecration of Holy Water

Solemn and Ancient Blessing

Prepare: cotta or alb, violet stole, a little salt in a dish, fresh water.

℣. Our help is in the name of the Lord.
℟. Who made heaven and earth.

Addressing the salt, the priest says:

I EXORCIZE you in the name of the living ✠ God, the true ✠ God, the holy ✠ God; the God who commanded that you be cast into the waters by the prophet Elisha to make stagnant water pure. Henceforth, be free from taint, and purifying to those who believe. Give health of mind and body to all partaking of you, and may evil fly from wherever you are sprinkled, together with all the cunning wiles of Satan. May every evil spirit flee at the command of the one who will come to judge the living and the dead, and the world by fire. Amen.

Let us pray.

ALMIGHTY and eternal God, we beseech you in your kindness and goodness to bless ✠ this salt which you have made for human use. Let it bring health of mind and body to all partaking of it. Let no corruption nor attack of the powers of evil approach anything touched or sprinkled with it. Through Christ our Lord. Amen.

Addressing the water, the priest says:

I EXORCIZE you in the name of God the Almighty ✠ Father, in the name of his Son ✠ Jesus Christ, our Lord, and in the strength of the Holy ✠ Spirit, that you may be pure water for the resisting of the enemy's power, and for his putting to flight with his rebellious angels, through the strength of the same Jesus Christ our Lord, who will come to judge the living and the dead, and the world by fire. Amen.

Let us pray.

O GOD, who made water the foundation of those rites that bring salvation to humankind, hear our prayers; pour forth your blessing ✠ into this purified water. May it be henceforth your instrument in the sacred rites, casting out the power of darkness, and warding off sickness, so that those places where it is sprinkled may be purified and freed from evil; no pestilential spirit shall take up his residence there, no breath of contagion touch it, but all the snares of the enemy shall be broken. And shall anything threaten the safety or peace of any person, may it flee at the touch of this water, that the health and prosperity sought by those invoking your name be shielded from all attacks. Through Christ our Lord. Amen.

The Roman Missal contains other texts for the blessing of water, but they are more suitable for Sundays, and in the presence of a congregation.

Candles
OTHER THAN AT CANDLEMAS

❧☩❧

A reading from the holy Gospel according to John.   8:12

JESUS spoke to the people, saying: I am the light of the world. The one who follows me does not walk in darkness, but shall have the light of life.

℣. Our help is in the name of the Lord.
℟. **Who made heaven and earth.**
℣. The Lord be with you.
℟. **And with your spirit.**

Let us pray.

LORD Jesus Christ, Son of the living God, we pray that you bless ✠ these candles (this candle) and by the sign of your holy cross make it a channel of your heavenly blessing that it may dispel the darkness of human minds: wherever these candles are (this candle is) lit or placed, may the powers of darkness tremble and flee in terror with all their minions, that all your disciples may walk in peace and safety. Who live and reign with the Father and the Holy Spirit, one God for ever and ever. Amen.

IMAGES

A reading from the letter of St Paul to the Colossians.   1:12–20

LET us give thanks to God the Father, who has made us worthy to be partakers of the inheritance of the saints in light: who has delivered us from the power of darkness and has transferred us into the kingdom of the Son whom he loves, in whom we have redemption through his blood, the remission of sins.

He is the image of the invisible God, the firstborn of all creation: for in him all things were created; in heaven and on earth, visible and invisible, whether thrones, or dominations, or principalities, or powers. All things were created by him and in him. And he is before all things: and in him all things hold together. He is the head of the body, the Church: the beginning, the firstborn from the dead, that in all things he may hold the primacy, for in him it has well pleased the Father that all fulness should dwell, and through him to reconcile all things to himself, making peace through the blood of his cross, both as to the things that are on earth and the things that are in heaven.

and/or

A reading from the holy Gospel according to John.   14:8–9

PHILIP said to Jesus: Lord, show us the Father; and we shall be satisfied. Jesus said to him: Have I been so long a time with you and have you not known me? Philip, whoever sees me sees the Father also.

An Image of our Lord

℣. Our help is in the name of the Lord.
℟. **Who made heaven and earth.**
℣. The Lord be with you.
℟. **And with your spirit.**

ALMIGHTY and eternal God, who do not forbid the making of images of your holy ones, so that as often as we look upon them with our eyes we may remember inwardly their deeds and their sanctity, and so learn to imitate them: we ask that you bless ✠ and sanctify this image made to call to mind your only-begotten Son, our Lord Jesus Christ; and grant to all who, in the presence of this image, humbly honour and call upon the help of your only Son, grace in this life and eternal glory in the next. Through the same Christ our Lord. Amen.

and/or

A LMIGHTY Father, look upon the face of your only-begotten Son, and on the intercession he makes with you on behalf of sinners. We ask you to bless ✠ this image, and grant that as we contemplate his face depicted here, we may become more like him in spirit, who lives and reigns with you and the Holy Spirit, one God for ever and ever. Amen.

An Image of our Lady

A LMIGHTY and eternal God, who do not forbid the making of images of your holy ones, so that as often as we look upon them with our eyes we may remember inwardly their deeds and their sanctity, and so learn to imitate them: we ask that you bless ✠ and sanctify this image made to call to mind and honour the memory of the most blessed Virgin Mary, mother of our Lord Jesus Christ; and grant to all who, in the presence of this image, honour and call upon the help of the Blessed Virgin, grace in this life and eternal glory in the next, by the merits of that same Blessed Virgin, and her power of intercession with you. Through the same Christ our Lord. Amen.

and/or

A LMIGHTY God, who looked upon your lowly handmaid the Blessed Virgin Mary, and whose Son, our Lord Jesus Christ, looked upon her face with love, we ask that you bless ✠ this image consecrated to her honour, and grant that as we contemplate her face on earth, we may one day see, love and honour it in heaven, where you live and reign for ever and ever. Amen.

An Image of a Saint

ALMIGHTY and eternal God, who do not forbid the making of images of your holy ones, so that as often as we look upon them with our eyes we may remember inwardly their deeds and their sanctity, and so learn to imitate them: we ask that you bless ✠ and sanctify this image made to call to mind and honour the memory of N. your Apostle (or Martyr, &c.), and grant to all who, in the presence of this image, honour and call upon the help of the same Saint N., grace in this life and eternal glory in the next, by the power of that same Apostle (or Martyr, &c.) and his/her power of intercession with you. Through the same Christ our Lord. Amen.

and/or

ALMIGHTY God, who have so graced the saints that they reflected something of your image and likeness upon earth, bless ✠, we pray, this image of Saint N., and grant that as we look upon it, we may be reminded of his/her virtues and holiness, and be inspired to imitate them. Through Christ our Lord. Amen.

Icons

Blessed be our God always, both now and ever, and unto ages of ages. Amen.

Holy God, holy and mighty, holy immortal one, have mercy upon us. *(Three times)*

An Icon of the Trinity or One of its Members

ALMIGHTY God and King of the Universe, who in the former dispensation forbade the making of images until the face of your only-begotten Son was revealed to the world in his most holy incarnation, bless and make holy this icon written to the honour of the most glorious and life-giving [*Trinity, or Son of God*], and grant that he whose image we venerate here below may grant us one day to contemplate in glory his ineffable beauty in truth, and to honour and adore him unto ages of ages. Amen.

Hallowed and blessed... *as below*

An Icon of a Saint or of the Mother of God

O LORD our God, who created us after your own image and likeness; who redeem us from our former corruption of the ancient curse through your Christ, the friend of mankind, who took upon himself the form of a servant and became man; who having taken upon himself our likeness remade your saints of the old covenant, and through whom also we are refashioned in the image of your pure blessedness: we venerate your saints as being in your image and likeness, and we adore and glorify you as our Creator; wherefore we pray you, send forth your blessing upon this icon, and with the sprinkling of hallowed water bless and make holy this icon unto your glory, in honour and remembrance of your Saint N. [or, the Mother of God]; and grant that this sanctification will be to all who venerate this icon of Saint N. [or, the Mother of God] and who standing before it send up their prayer unto you. Through the grace and bounties and love of your only-begotten Son, with whom you are blessed together with your all-holy, good and life-giving Spirit, both now and ever, and unto ages of ages. Amen.

Sprinkling the icon with holy water in the form of a cross, he says:

HALLOWED and blessed be this icon of Saint N. [or, the Mother of God], by the grace of the Holy Spirit, through the sprinkling of holy water; in the name of the ✠ Father, and of the ✠ Son, and of the Holy ✠ Spirit. Amen.

Some consecrate an icon with Chrism, which is applied to the reverse in five crosses to the corners and the centre:

THIS sacred icon, written to the glory of God and of Saint N. [*or the Mother of God*] is consecrated to the devotion of N. [*the place where, or the person by whom it is to be prayed before*], in the name of the Father, and of the Son, and of the Holy Spirit. Amen.

ANY DEVOTIONAL OBJECT

A LMIGHTY God, whose only-begotten Son took flesh and was born of the Virgin Mary into this material world, thereby making creation holy and a means of grace: sanctify ✠ also this N. / article of faith, that it may be to those who see or use it an inspiration to prayer, to the seeking of your face and to the keeping of your commandments. Through our Lord Jesus Christ your Son, who lives and reigns with you in the unity of the Holy Spirit, one God for ever and ever. Amen.

GIFTS TO THE CHURCH

A reading from the second letter of St Paul to the Corinthians.　　9:8–11

G OD is able to give you every blessing in abundance, so that, having everything you need, you may always have enough in abundance for every good work. As it is written: He has dispersed abroad, he has given to the poor: his justice remains for ever. And he who gives the seed to the sower, will both give you bread to eat, and will multiply your seed, and increase the growth of the fruits of your justice. So, being enriched in all things, you may abound in generosity, which through us gives thanks to God.

A LMIGHTY God, giver of all good things, we thank you for your generous bounty towards us, and it is our greatest joy to return to your service this token of our love for you. We ask you to bless this ... which we now dedicate to your service: Father, Son ✠ and Holy Spirit. Amen.

ROSARIES

TO the praise and glory of the Virgin Mary, Mother of God, and in memory of the life, death and resurrection of her Son, our Lord Jesus Christ, may this rosary (these rosaries) be blessed and sanctified in the name of the Father, and of the Son, ✠ and of the Holy Spirit. Amen.

℣. Our help is in the name of the Lord.
℟. **Who made heaven and earth.**
℣. The Lord be with you.
℟. **And with your spirit.**

Let us pray.

ALMIGHTY and merciful God, who from the depths of the kindness with which you have loved us willed that at the message of an angel your only-begotten Son should descend from heaven to earth, to the most holy womb of our Lady, the most Blessed Virgin Mary, and that he should take flesh, experience death on the cross, and rise again gloriously on the third day, all to free us from the power of the devil: we beseech your great mercy that this rosary (these rosaries) which your Church brings to you for consecration to the honour and praise of the same Mother of your Son may by you be blessed ✠, sanctified, and filled with the power of the Holy Spirit, that whoever carries it/them, keeps it/them reverently in their homes and prays with it/them, contemplating the divine mysteries, may enjoy sweet and persevering devotion, and may be sharers in the graces that our Lord and Saviour has won for us; may they be freed from all harm, both seen and unseen, in this age, and at the end of their earthly pilgrimage, full of good works, may they be found worthy to be welcomed into heaven by the Blessed Virgin Mary, Mother of God herself. Through the same Christ our Lord. Amen.

21

ARTICLES FOR PARTICULAR DEVOTIONS

Formerly some of these articles had to be blessed by a priest of a particular religious order. Now, any priest in good standing may do so.

The Brown Scapular of our Lady of Mount Carmel

༄༅ ⚓ ༄༅

Blessing and Enrolment

℣. Show us, O Lord, your mercy.
℟. **And grant us your salvation.**
℣. O Lord hear my prayer.
℟. **And let my cry come to you.**
℣. The Lord be with you.
℟. **And with your spirit.**

Let us pray.

LORD Jesus Christ, Saviour of mankind, by your right hand sanctify ✠ these scapulars (this scapular) which your servants will devoutly wear for the love of you and of your Mother, the Blessed Virgin Mary of Mount Carmel; so that, by her intercession, they may be protected from the wickedness of the enemy and persevere in your grace until death. Who live and reign for ever and ever. Amen.

The scapulars are then sprinkled with holy water, and each is placed on its recipient, the priest saying:

RECEIVE this blessed Scapular and ask the most holy Virgin that, by her merits, it may be worn with no stain of sin, and may protect you from all harm, and bring you into everlasting life. Amen.

By the power granted to me, I admit you to a share in all the spiritual works performed, with the merciful help of Jesus Christ, by the Religious of Mount Carmel: in the name of the Father, and of the Son, ✠ and of the Holy Spirit. Amen.

MAY Almighty God, Creator of heaven and earth, bless ✠ you whom he has been pleased to receive into the Confraternity of the Blessed Virgin Mary of Mount Carmel. We beg her to crush the head of the ancient serpent in the hour of your death, and, in the end, to obtain for you a palm and the crown of your everlasting inheritance. Through Christ our Lord. Amen.

THE MIRACULOUS MEDAL

BLESSING AND IMPOSITION

℣. Our help is in the name of the Lord.
℟. **Who made heaven and earth.**
℣. The Lord be with you.
℟. **And with your spirit.**

Let us pray.

ALMIGHTY and merciful God, who have granted by the many apparitions of the Immaculate Virgin Mary on earth a wonderful help to the salvation of the human race: we ask you to graciously pour out your blessing ✠ on this medal (these medals); that whoever piously and devotedly wears it (them) may know your protection and may receive your mercy. Through Christ our Lord. Amen.

The medals are sprinkled with holy water, and then imposed on the wearer with this prayer:

RECEIVE this holy medal and wear it faithfully, and strive to be worthy of it: and may the most holy and Immaculate Lady of Heaven protect and defend you, multiplying again the wonders of her holiness, adding her prayers to yours in whatever you seek from God, that whether in life or death, you may rest in her most tender and maternal arms. Amen.

23

Lord, have mercy.
Christ, have mercy.
Lord, have mercy.

Our Father ...

℣. Queen conceived without original sin,
℟. Pray for us.
℣. O Lord hear my prayer.
℟. And let my cry come to you.
℣. The Lord be with you.
℟. And with your spirit.

Let us pray.

LORD Jesus Christ, who will that your most blessed mother, immaculate from the beginning, should be glorified with innumerable miracles: grant that as we continually beg her protection, we may come to experience eternal joy. Who live and reign for ever and ever. Amen.

THE MEDAL OF ST BENEDICT

BLESSING AND IMPOSITION

℣. Our help is in the name of the Lord.
℟. Who made heaven and earth.
℣. The Lord be with you.
℟. And with your spirit.

IN the name of God the Father ✠ almighty, who made heaven and earth, the seas and all that they contain, I exorcise this medal (these medals) against the power and attacks of the evil one. May all who prayerfully make use of it (them) be blessed with health in soul and body. In the name of the Father ✠ almighty, of his Son ✠ Jesus Christ our Lord, and of the Holy ✠ Spirit the Paraclete, and in the love of the same Lord Jesus Christ who will come on the last day to judge the living and the dead, and the world by fire. Amen.

Let us pray.

A LMIGHTY God, boundless source of all that is good, we humbly pray that, through the intercession of St Benedict, you pour out your ✠ blessing on this medal (these medals). May those who make use of it (them) with sincerity and devotion, and who are persistent in doing good works, deserve to receive health of mind and body, the grace of sanctification and the indulgences attached to this devotion. With the aid of your mercy, may he (she, they) also resist all the deceits and traps of the devil, and one day merit to appear in your sight pure and holy. Through Christ our Lord. Amen.

The Chaplet of our Lady of Sorrows

T O the praise and glory of the Virgin Mary, Mother of God, and in memory of the sorrows she bore during the life and death of her Son our Lord Jesus Christ, may this chaplet be blessed ✠ and sanctified ✠ in the name of the Father, and of ✠ the Son, and of the Holy Spirit. Amen.

CROSSES

A reading from the letter of St Paul to the Galatians. 6:14ff

GOD forbid that I should glory, save in the cross of our Lord Jesus Christ, by whom the world is crucified to me, and I to the world ... From henceforth let no man be troublesome to me; for I bear the marks of the Lord Jesus in my body. The grace of our Lord Jesus Christ be with your spirit, brethren. Amen.

A Cross for Wearing

℣. We adore you, O Christ, and we bless you.
℟. **Because by your holy Cross you have redeemed the world.**
℣. The Lord be with you.
℟. **And with your spirit.**

Let us pray.

HOLY Father, almighty and eternal God, we pray that you bless ✠ this remembrance of your cross, that through it the human race may once more be given wholeness, strength of faith, abundance of good works, and salvation of souls; may it be a solace and a protection and a defence against the wicked assaults of the enemy. Through Christ our Lord. Amen.

A Cross for Devotion

℣. We adore you, O Christ, and we bless you.
℟. **Because by your holy Cross you have redeemed the world.**
℣. The Lord be with you.
℟. **And with your spirit.**

Let us pray.

LORD Jesus Christ, we ask that you bless this cross, sign of that cross by which you freed the world from the power of the devil, and on which you overcame, by your passion, the one who first inspired sin and who rejoiced at the fall of humankind when they tasted of the tree. May this cross be sanctified in the name of the Father, and of the Son, ✠ and of the Holy Spirit, that whoever prays before it in your honour may find health and wholeness for body and soul. Who live and reign for ever and ever. Amen.

Placing of a Cross in a Public Space

If possible, the priest should hold the cross, and make the blessing with it.

℣. We adore you, O Christ, and we bless you.
℟. Because by your holy Cross you have redeemed the world.
℣. The Lord be with you.
℟. And with your spirit.

Let us pray.

MAY this place be blessed ✠ and sanctified, Lord God, by the cross of your only-begotten Son our Lord Jesus Christ. Let no evil enter into this place which we consecrate to your glory. At the sight of this cross let Satan and his minions flee, and may your holy angels who praise you day and night take up their place and join with us in for ever singing your glory in heaven, where you live and reign for ever and ever. Amen.

If practicable, the cross is now enthroned in its place.

A Processional Cross
SEE P. 56

CONSECRATION OF PEOPLE
TO THE SACRED HEART

Public Consecration to
the Sacred Heart in Church

This consecration was first composed by Pope Leo XIII and has been customarily prayed before the Blessed Sacrament exposed. It can be used together with the Litany of the Sacred Heart.

O MOST sweet Jesus, Redeemer of mankind, behold us prostrate most humbly before thine altar. Thine we are; thine we wish to be; and that we may be united to thee more closely, behold we, each of us, by his own free act consecrates himself this day to thy most Sacred Heart.

Many there are, indeed, who have never known thee: many, despising thy commands, have rejected thee. Have pity on them all, most merciful Jesus, and draw them to thy sacred heart. Be King, O Lord, not only over the faithful who have never strayed from thee; but over those prodigal children also who have forsaken thee. Make them return in haste to their Father's home, lest through misery and want they perish. Be King over those who have been misled by error or who are divided from us by schism, and call them back to the haven of truth and unity of faith, that soon there may be one fold and one Shepherd. Be King, then, over all who are sunk in superstition, and tarry not to bring them out of darkness into God's light and kingdom.

Grant to thy Church, O Lord, safety and sure liberty; grant to all nations the peace that comes of order; and over all the earth from pole to pole make this one chant resound: Praise be to the divine heart through which was wrought for us salvation; to it be glory and honour for ever and ever. Amen.

Ritus Servandus

Individual Consecration
to the Sacred Heart

There is no reason why this form should not be used by a group in church as a more modern alternative to the above. It needs little alteration.

I, N. N. , give myself and consecrate to the Sacred Heart of our Lord Jesus Christ, my person and my life, my actions, pains and sufferings, so that I may be unwilling to make use of any part of my being save to honour, love, and glorify the Sacred Heart. This is my unchanging purpose, namely, to be all his, and to do all things for the love of him, at the same time renouncing with all my heart whatever is displeasing to him. I therefore take you, O Sacred Heart, to be the only object of my love, the guardian of my life, my assurance of salvation, the remedy of my weakness and inconstancy, the atonement for all the faults of my life, and my sure refuge at the hour of death. Be then, O Heart of goodness, my justification before God our Father, and turn away from me his justified anger. O Heart of love, I put all my confidence in you, for I fear everything from my own wickedness and frailty, but I hope for all things from your goodness and bounty. Consume in me all that displeases you or resists your holy will; let your pure love imprint itself so deeply on my heart, that I shall never be able to forget or to be separated from you. May I obtain from your loving kindness the grace of having my name written on your heart, for in you I desire to place all my happiness and all my glory, living and dying in your true service.

St Margaret Mary Alacoque

Enthronement of an Image
of the Sacred Heart in a Home
and the Consecration of a Family

℣. Our help is in the name of the Lord.
℞. Who made heaven and earth.
℣. The Lord be with you.
℞. And with your spirit.

Let us pray.

A LMIGHTY, ever living God we ask you to bless ✠ this image of the Sacred Heart of your well-beloved Son our Lord Jesus Christ and bless the home in which it is enthroned, and the family who desire to honour that Sacred Heart in their lives. Through the same Christ our Lord. Amen.

The image may then be enthroned or unveiled:
Behold the Heart which has loved the world so much.

It is customary at this point to recite the Apostles' Creed. The following act of consecration could be read by all together, or by one member of the family (ideally whoever fulfils the role of head of the household) or by the priest on their behalf.

M OST Sacred Heart of Jesus, since you revealed to St Margaret Mary your desire to be the King of Christian families, behold, in order to please you, we stand here before you today to acknowledge your rule over this home of ours. From now on we desire to live your life; we desire all the virtues to flourish in our family, and we wish to cast from us that spirit of worldliness that you abhor. Reign over our minds, we pray, by our simple faith, and over our hearts by the special burning love given to you alone, which we will renew often by our worthy reception of Holy Communion.

Most Sacred Heart, we ask you to preside over us whenever we come together; bless all our spiritual and temporal duties, help us to solve whatever problems come our way; make our joys holy, and comfort our sorrows. Should any of us ever grieve you, fill that one with confidence in your forgiving mercy for the repentant sinner. And when death shall come to divide and bring us sorrow, give us the gift of resignation to your most holy will, and strengthen our faith that we shall all be united again in heaven to sing of your glory and goodness for ever.

Our Blessed Mother and St Joseph, we pray that you present this consecration to our Blessed Lord and keep the memory of it fresh in our minds to the end of our lives.

Praise to the Sacred Heart that wrought our salvation! To it be honour and glory for ever and ever. Amen.

BOOKS

⋘⚓⋙

Missals

A reading from the first letter of St Paul to the Corinthians.   11:23–26

FOR I have received from the Lord what I also delivered to you, that the Lord Jesus, on the same night in which he was betrayed, took bread. And giving thanks, he broke it and said: Take, and eat: this is my body, which shall be given up for you: do this for the commemoration of me. In the same manner also he took the cup, after he had eaten, saying: This cup is the new testament in my blood: do this, as often as you shall drink it, for the commemoration of me. For as often as you shall eat this bread, and drink this cup, you shall proclaim the death of the Lord, until he comes.

Let us pray.

LORD Jesus Christ, who have commanded us to celebrate the Eucharist in your memory, bless ✠, we pray, this missal dedicated to the fulfilling of your command. May the meaning of the mystery of your Body and Blood penetrate ever more deeply into our hearts, that our reverence and awe at this heavenly banquet may grow ever stronger as we journey towards that kingdom where you reign with the Father and the Holy Spirit, one God for ever and ever. Amen.

PERSONAL MISSAL

ALMIGHTY and eternal God, we pray that you bless ✠ this missal and the one who will use it. May we all grow in our understanding of the liturgy as the source and summit of the Christian life, being enabled to achieve a conscious and real participation in the celebration of the most glorious Sacrifice of the Mass. As you give your Son to us, may we be inspired, by reading your word and receiving his body and blood, to give ourselves unreservedly to you and our neighbour. Through the same Christ our Lord. Amen.

A Bible or Lectionary

A reading from the letter of St James. 1:21–25

CASTING away all uncleanness and abundance of wickedness, with meekness receive the implanted word, which is able to save your souls. And be doers of the word and not hearers only, deceiving yourselves. For if a man be a hearer of the word and not a doer, he is like a person seeing his own face in a mirror; he observes himself and goes his way, soon forgetting what manner of person he is. But the one who has looked into the perfect law of liberty and has continued in it, not becoming a forgetful hearer but a doer of those acts: he shall be blessed in what he does.

ALMIGHTY God, who have sent your Son into the world as the Word made flesh, grant that we may read and meditate upon your holy word as we see it in the scriptures. Enlighten our minds, warm our hearts to believe what you have spoken, and grant us an ever deeper love of you and your commandments, through your Word, Jesus Christ our Lord. Amen.

May this Bible/Lectionary, and all who find the Word of God in it be blessed in the name of the Father, and of the Son, ✠ and of the Holy Spirit. Amen.

Prayer Books

A reading from the book of Psalms. 40:7–9 (39:8–10)

I SAID: Behold, I come. In the beginning of the book it is written of me that I should do your will; O God, I have desired it, and your law is in the midst of my heart. I have declared your justice in the great assembly, I will not restrain my lips: O Lord, you know it.

HOLY Father, we consecrate this book (these books) to your praise, and we pray that you bless ✠ it (them), that those who will use it (them) may grow in your knowledge and service, and one day come to see and praise you in your glory, where you live and reign with your Son and the Holy Spirit, one God for ever and ever. Amen.

Service Books

A reading from the letter of St Paul to the Colossians.   3:15–17

LET the peace of Christ rejoice in your hearts, in which you are called in one body: and be thankful. Let the word of Christ dwell in you abundantly, in all wisdom: teaching and admonishing one another in psalms, hymns, and spiritual canticles, singing with grace in your hearts to God. All whatsoever you do in word or in work, do all in the name of the Lord Jesus Christ, giving thanks to God the Father through him.

HEAVENLY Father, worshipped by all the heavenly hosts, we ask your blessing upon this congregation and upon these ✠ books which we dedicate to your service. May our worship here on earth, though but a pale reflection of the great liturgy of heaven, nonetheless be pleasing to you and helpful to our salvation. We ask this through Christ our Lord. Amen.

Hymn Books

A reading from the letter of St Paul to the Colossians.   3:15–17

LET the peace of Christ rejoice in your hearts, in which you are called in one body: and be thankful. Let the word of Christ dwell in you abundantly, in all wisdom: teaching and admonishing one another in psalms, hymns, and spiritual canticles, singing with grace in your hearts to God. All whatsoever you do in word or in work, do all in the name of the Lord Jesus Christ, giving thanks to God the Father through him.

LORD God, your Church loves to sing your praise in her psalms and with hymns. We ask you to bless ✠ these hymn books and those who will use them, that they might sing with the Spirit and with understanding, and may make a joyful noise to you, O Lord, who live and reign for ever and ever. Amen.

Dominic Jacob

THE DECEASED

A New Cemetery

If possible, a permanent crucifix should be erected in the new cemetery. If this be not possible, a crucifix should be brought for the occasion, perhaps a processional one. The priest, standing before the crucifix, says:

Let us pray.

ALMIGHTY God, the guardian of our souls, protector of our salvation and the strength of believers, look kindly on our humble prayers, and, as we enter here for the first time, bless and ✠ sanctify this cemetery, that those whose bodies will lie here when the course of their life is done may in the great judgment day come to eternal life and joy with the blessed. Through Christ our Lord. Amen.

The Great Litany is now said or sung (see p. 153), and after the invocation That you might free our souls ... *the following invocation is added in by the priest:*

That you might sanctify and ✠ bless this cemetery,
Hear us, Lord, we pray.

The entire cemetery is now blessed with holy water. When this has finished, the priest says the following prayer before the cross:

Let us pray.

O GOD, Creator of the entire world, restorer of the human race and perfect director of all creatures visible and invisible: we humbly pray with voices and pure hearts that you may purify ✠, bless ✠ and sanctify ✠ this cemetery, in which, after the journey of this life, the bodies of your servants will lie at rest; grant in your great mercy to those who have placed their trust in you the remission of all their sins; and likewise grant eternal consolation to those whose bodies will lie here peacefully awaiting that first Archangel's clarion call to arise. Through Christ our Lord. Amen.

A Garden for the Burial of Ashes

SINCE we know that we all must die, let us pray that Almighty God, to whom all people are alive, will bless this resting place among us and bring to life once more all those whose remains will rest here.

A reading from the letter of St Paul to the Romans.   6:3–5, 8–9

DO you not know that all of us who are baptized in Christ Jesus are baptized into his death? We were buried together with him by baptism into death; so that as Christ was raised from the dead by the glory of the Father, so we too may walk in newness of life. If we have been planted together in the likeness of his death, we shall also share in the likeness of his resurrection. Now if we have died with Christ, we believe that we shall also come to life together with Christ: for we know that Christ, having risen from the dead, will die no more; death shall no more have dominion over him. For having died to sin, he died once; but now living, he lives to God.

Let us pray.

O GOD, who created the human race from the dust of the earth, and commanded that we should return to the dust from which we came: mercifully grant our prayers for the souls of all those whose ashes will lie here awaiting the day of resurrection. May this place be a solace for those who mourn, a place where they may find peace and increased faith that one day they will be reunited with the souls and bodies of those whom they have loved and lost a while. Through Christ our Lord. Amen.

May the Lord God bless this garden of prayer and remembrance and make it holy: the Father, the Son ✠ and the Holy Spirit.

A Gravestone or Memorial

Let us pray.

O GOD, who made the grave a bed of rest and hope for those whose bodies are subject to decay, hear our prayers for the souls of your servants who have departed this life, and particularly for N. in whose memory we consecrate this memorial. May it remind us of the one we have loved, and strengthen our faith and hope in the resurrection of the dead when we shall look upon the face of N. once more, our bodies glorified and transformed into the likeness of him in whose image we were made, our Lord Jesus Christ, who lives and reigns for ever and ever. Amen.

A Memorial Plant or Tree

Let us pray.

O CHRIST, the true seed buried in the earth to rise again once more, we consecrate this [*plant or tree*] to your glory and to the memory of N. Grant that his/her memory may stay fresh and green in our minds and hearts and grow with this [*plant or tree*] into a thing of beauty, bringing joy into the lives of many. May the inspiration N. brought to our lives live on in us, that the work he/she did may continue to grow and bear fruit in the world which he/she has now left to flourish with you in your glory, where you live and reign for ever and ever. Amen.

May this [*plant or tree*] grow strong to beautify this place and comfort our hearts, in the name of the Father, the Son ✠ and the Holy Spirit. Amen.

Blessing of Graves on All Souls' Day
SEE P. 211

PART II

BLESSINGS

Those things which form a part of our daily lives, and which we dedicate to the Lord for the time they will be in our possession.

THE BLESSING OF A HOUSE

A reading from the holy Gospel according to Luke. 10:38–42

NOW it came to pass as they travelled, that Jesus entered a certain town: and a woman named Martha received him into her house. And she had a sister called Mary, who, sitting at the Lord's feet, heard his word. But Martha was busy with much serving. She stood and said: Lord, do you not care that my sister has left me alone to serve? Speak to her, therefore, that she might help me. And the Lord answering, said to her: Martha, Martha, you are anxious and troubled about many things, but only one thing is necessary. Mary has chosen the best part, which shall not be taken away from her.

LONGER FORM

℣. Peace be to this place
℟. **And to all who dwell here.**

It is customary to sprinkle each room with holy water as it is visited.

IN THE ENTRANCE HALL

The Lord bless ✠ your going out and your coming in from this day forth and for ever. Amen.

ALMIGHTY God, our most welcome visitor, bless the entrance of this home. May those who cross this threshold in peace find within a ready welcome and an open heart. May this door keep out all sin and evil, so that within there may be only goodness and truth, and the presence of your kingdom. Through Christ our Lord. Amen.

IN THE MAIN ROOM OF THE HOUSE

LORD Jesus Christ, who found a ready welcome in the house of Martha and Mary, grant that in this room may be much laughter and good nature. May dissension never gain a foothold here, but may this place be to all a foretaste of heaven, where all people will enjoy each other's company in the communion of saints, praising God for ever and ever. Amen.

IN THE KITCHEN

TEACH us, good Lord, to grow in humility, and in the practical love of our fellow human beings. In this kitchen may we learn that it is truly more blessed to serve than to be served, and that fidelity and affection are most truly learnt in the simplest ways. We ask this through Christ our Lord. Amen.

IN THE DINING ROOM

IN this room, O Lord, give us a foretaste of your heavenly banquet, where none goes hungry, where none goes lonely, but all is satisfaction and joy. Grace this table with your blessing, Lord, and accept our thanks for what has been and will be received by those who sit here. We ask this through Christ our Lord. Amen.

ON THE STAIRS

O LORD, who never allow the steps of the just to stumble, keep all who use these stairs safe. May they ascend also in the path of virtue, and thereby come eventually to heaven. We ask this through Christ our Lord. Amen.

IN A MARRIED BEDROOM

BLESS this room, O Lord, where we remember the joy of the wedding day. Renew the grace of marriage, and move those who sleep here to the keeping of your commandments in the truest bond of love. We ask this through Christ our Lord. Amen.

IN A SINGLE BEDROOM

GUARD our purity, O blessed Lord, and bless our sleep. Make us quick to keep your commandments, that when we finally fall asleep in death we may wake to eternal glory. Through Christ our Lord. Amen.

IN THE BATHROOM

WASH us, O Lord, and we will be truly clean. In this room, O Lord Jesus, may we remember the washing of baptism which brought us eternal life, and may we remember your words that inner cleanliness is more important than outer. Let us set aside vanity and self-centredness, and make us fit citizens of your kingdom, where you live and reign for ever and ever. Amen.

IN THE PRINCIPAL ROOM ONCE MORE

MOST blessed Trinity: we consecrate this home to your honour and glory. May it become for all who dwell here the place wherein they find the means of salvation. Mary, Mother of God, be a mother in this house: angels and saints, protect all who enter or dwell here with your powerful intercession.

Our Father.

Hail Mary.

℣. The Lord be with you.
℟. And with your spirit.

Let us pray.

VISIT this house, O Lord, we pray, and drive far from it the deadly power of the enemy. May your holy angels dwell here instead, that we may be preserved in peace, with your blessing on us always. Through our Lord Jesus Christ your Son, who lives and reigns with you and the Holy Spirit, one God for ever and ever. Amen.

℣. The Lord be with you.
℟. And with your spirit.

May Almighty God bless this house and all who dwell here, the Father, the Son ✠ and the Holy Spirit. Amen.

Blessing of a House
(shorter, traditional, form)

Asperges me
Sprinkle me, O Lord with hyssop and I shall be truly clean; wash me, and I shall be whiter than snow.

All rooms are sprinkled with holy water.

℣. O Lord, hear my prayer.
℞. **And let my cry come to you.**
℣. The Lord be with you.
℞. **And with your spirit.**

Let us pray.

HEAR us, Lord, holy almighty and eternal God, and send your holy angel from heaven to visit, protect, bless and defend this place and all who dwell in it. Through Christ our Lord. Amen.

℣. The Lord be with you.
℞. **And with your spirit.**

May Almighty God bless this house and all who dwell here, the Father, the Son ✠ and the Holy Spirit. Amen.

A very short blessing prayer

MAY the peaceful light of your fatherly gaze enlighten this home. May the fulness of your blessing come upon all who live here, that while they live here safe and sound in this house which human hands have made, their hearts too may be your home. Amen.

Gelasian Sacramentary

Blessing of a House
(another shorter form)

℣. O Lord, hear my prayer.
℟. And let my cry come to you.
℣. The Lord be with you.
℟. And with your spirit.

Let us pray.

B LESS ✠ O Lord, almighty God, this house, that here there may be health, chasteness, wholeness, strength, humility, goodness and generosity, the fulfilment of the commandments, and thanksgiving to God, Father, Son and Holy Spirit; and so may his blessing remain on this house and all who dwell here, now and for ever. Amen.

The house is sprinkled with holy water.

Blessing of a House in Eastertide

℣. Peace be to this place.
℟. And to all who dwell here.

This blessing should ideally use water blessed for baptisms at the Easter Vigil, diluted if necessary.

Vidi Aquam
I saw water flowing from the right side of the temple, alleluia, and all who came to this water were saved, alleluia, alleluia.

Each room is sprinkled with the Easter water.

℣. Show us, O Lord, your mercy, alleluia.
℟. And grant us your salvation, alleluia.

℣. O Lord, hear my prayer.
℟. **And let my cry come to you.**
℣. The Lord be with you.
℟. **And with your spirit.**

Let us pray.

A LMIGHTY Father, holy God, hear our prayers, who commanded the houses of the Hebrews to be marked with the blood of
the paschal lamb as a protection from the avenging angel, thus
prefiguring Christ the true Lamb of God, and the Christian Passover of
his death and resurrection; we pray that you send your holy angel from
heaven to visit, protect, bless and defend this place and all who dwell in
it. Through Christ our Lord. Amen.

℣. The Lord be with you.
℟. **And with your spirit.**

May Almighty God bless this house and all who dwell here, the Father,
the Son ✠ and the Holy Spirit. Amen.

Blessing of a Newly-built House
Paraphrased from a German ritual of 1685

℣. Our help is in the name of the Lord.
℟. **Who made heaven and earth.**
℣. The Lord be with you.
℟. **And with your spirit.**

Let us pray.

A LMIGHTY God, who have made the priesthood a channel
among many others of great grace, we pray you that by my visit
to this place whatever needs to be blessed will be blessed and
that you will extend your powerful right hand and that as I enter this
house, the merits and intercessions of the saints may accompany me
that the devils might flee and angels of peace take up their abode here.
Through Christ our Lord. Amen.

LORD, holy Father, by the merits of your Son, our Lady (and Saint N. the patron of our parish), bless ✠ this house, as you blessed the houses of our forefathers Abraham, Isaac and Jacob. And, Lord Jesus Christ, who commanded your disciples, on entering a house to say 'Peace be to this house': may your peace be upon this house, upon all those who live here, and upon all those who will live here in the future; keep them untrammelled and happy; fill them a hundredfold with wine and oil and and bring them finally to glory. Through Christ our Lord. Amen.

BLESS, ✠ Lord, this home; its land and its buildings and grant that here may be found health, holiness, strength and glory, together with humility, goodness, patience, gentleness and the fulness of the law's observance, obedient to God the Father, Son and Holy Spirit whom we ask to bless this place and all who dwell herein. May the holy angels of God come down to this place and defend it, protect it from all evil and its agents, for the eternal holiness of God's name. Keep this place undefiled for ever, Lord, since it has now been purified, blessed and sanctified; send out the stream of your grace onto this home from your eternal home on high, that your mercy might flow like a fountain, and bid your avenging angel to stay his hand; let his glory appear, and bid him bless this house. Holy Mary, I invoke your protection on this house and land; fill it with your blessing for you are the merciful mother and the comforter of the afflicted. Holy Father/Mother St N. arise, and by the passion of our Lord Jesus Christ bless ✠ and sanctify this house and land, that the devil and his wicked angels might not rejoice, neither stand in this place. And I, priest of Jesus Christ and servant of God in his name cast out and annihilate every doer of evil or fiend from this place, in the name of the Father, and of the Son, ✠ and of the Holy Spirit. Amen.

MAY the peace and blessing ✠ of the Holy Trinity, and the patronage of St N. descend on this place, and may those who dwell here pray devotedly, sweetly sleep, eat, drink and do all other things in peace. Through Christ our Lord. Amen.

Blessing of a House

Where People Are Troubled
By Things That Go Bump in the Night

This blessing is a simple one against worries about evil. If greater distur-bance is suspected, the proper authorities should be approached.

℣. Peace be to this place.
℟. And to all who dwell here.

A LMIGHTY God, our sure refuge and defence, we pray for all whose who live in this place, that they may be protected against all the assaults of any persons, bodily or spiritual, who might harm them. Send your holy angels to dwell here and befriend those who live here. Comfort them in their concerns and grant them your peace, who live and reign for ever and ever. Amen.

All may say at this point the prayer to St Michael:

H OLY Michael Archangel, defend us in the day of battle. Be our safe-guard against the wickedness and snares of the enemy. May God rebuke him, we humbly pray, and do thou, Prince of the heavenly host, by the power of God, thrust down to hell Satan and all wicked spirits who wander this world for the ruin of souls. Amen.

All the house should now be sprinkled with holy water, and may be conse-crated to the Sacred Heart (see p. 30).

℣. O Lord, hear my prayer.
℟. And let my cry come to you.
℣. The Lord be with you.
℟. And with your spirit.

Let us pray.

H EAR us, Lord, holy almighty and eternal God, and send your holy angel from heaven to visit, protect, bless and defend this place and all who dwell in it. Through Christ our Lord. Amen.

℣. The Lord be with you.
℟. And with your spirit.

May Almighty God bless and protect this house and all who dwell here, the Father, the Son ✠ and the Holy Spirit. Amen.

BLESSING OF A HOUSE AT EPIPHANY

SEE P. 185

THE BLESSING OF AN ORATORY
OR PRIVATE PRAYER SPACE

A reading from the holy Gospel according to Luke.   5:15–16

THE fame of Jesus went abroad all the more, and great crowds came together to listen, and to be healed by him of their infirmities. But he retired into the desert, and prayed.

℣. O Lord, hear my prayer.
℟. **And let my cry come to you.**
℣. The Lord be with you.
℟. **And with your spirit.**

Let us pray.

LORD God, whose Son Jesus Christ our Lord repeated your words that 'my house shall be a house of prayer,' bless ✠, we pray, this place of prayer, set apart as a retreat for us to be alone with you. Here may we sit at the Lord's feet as did Mary, sister of Lazarus; here may we come to know him as our dearest friend and our most loving Saviour. Here may we learn to listen, to pray, and to love as you love. Through the same Jesus Christ our Lord. Amen.

Holy water

MEALTIMES

Formal Grace before Meals

℣. Bless the Lord.
℟. Bless the Lord.

At midday meal

The eyes of all look to you, O Lord, and you grant them food when it is needed. You open wide your hand and fill all your creatures with blessings.

At evening meal

The poor shall eat and have their fill, and shall praise the Lord who has blessed them, for they will live for ever and ever.

Lord, have mercy.
Christ, have mercy.
Lord, have mercy.

Our Father.

Let us pray.

BLESS us, O ✠ Lord, and these your gifts which we are about to receive from your bounty. Through Christ our Lord. Amen.

At midday meal

May the King of eternal glory make us partakers one day of his heavenly banquet. Amen.

At evening meal

May the King of eternal glory draw us to share in the banquet of everlasting life. Amen.

Formal Grace After Meals

AFTER MIDDAY MEAL

All your works, O Lord, proclaim your goodness. And all your holy people rejoice in you.

AFTER EVENING MEAL

The good and merciful Lord has caused us to remember his goodness.

WE GIVE you thanks, O Lord, for all your benefits, who live and reign for ever and ever. Amen.

Psalm 116

PRAISE the Lord, all you nations,
Praise him, all you peoples.
For his mercy has been shown forth towards us,
And the Lord keeps his word for ever.
Glory be …

Lord, have mercy.
Christ, have mercy.
Lord, have mercy.

Our Father.

℣. The Lord gives freely to the poor.
℟. **And his justice shall last for ever.**
℣. I will bless the Lord at all times.
℟. **His praise shall be always on my lips.**
℣. My soul will ever praise the Lord.
℟. **The redeemed shall hear it and be glad.**
℣. Bless the Lord with me.
℟. **Let us praise his name together.**
℣. May the name of the Lord be blessed.
℟. **Now and for evermore.**

R EWARD, O Lord, with eternal life all those who have been good to
us, for the sake of your holy name. Amen.

℣. Let us bless the Lord.
℟. **Thanks be to God.**

May the souls of the faithful departed, through the mercy of God, rest
in peace. Amen.

Simple Grace before meals

B LESS ✠ us, Lord, and these your gifts which we are about to receive
from your bounty. Through Christ our Lord. Amen.

or

L ORD, bless ✠ this meal, those who have prepared it, and give food
to the hungry. Amen.

Simple Grace after meals

W E give you thanks, almighty God, for these and all your benefits,
who live and reign for ever and ever. Amen.

May the souls of the faithful ✠ departed, through the mercy of God
rest in peace. Amen.

or

W E thank you, Lord, for the food we have received. Make us generous to those in want, and always grateful for what you have given
us. Through Christ our Lord. Amen.

MUSICAL INSTRUMENTS

❧ ✠ ❧

Blessing of an Organ

℣. Our help is in the name of the Lord.
℟. Who made heaven and earth.

Psalm 150

PRAISE the Lord in his holy places:
praise him in the firmament of his power.
praise him for his mighty acts,
praise him according to the excellence of his greatness.

Praise him with the sound of trumpet,
praise him with psaltery and harp.
Praise him with timbrel and choir,
praise him with strings and organs.

Praise him on high-sounding cymbals,
praise him on cymbals of joy.

Let everything that breathes praise the Lord!

Glory be ...

℣. The Lord be with you.
℟. And with your spirit.

Let us pray.

ALMIGHTY God, who through Moses your servant caused trumpets to sound at the sacrifices offered to the glory of your name, and willed that the children of Israel should sing your praise with instruments of joy; bless ✠, we pray, this organ dedicated to your worship and grant that the faithful who sing joyfully to its leading here on earth may be led to sing your praise in the eternal rejoicing of heaven. Through our Lord Jesus Christ your Son, who lives and reigns with you and the Holy Spirit, one God for ever and ever. Amen.

Another Blessing of an Organ

HEAVENLY Father, who take delight that your children should praise you with joy, bless ✠ this organ, and grant that its voice may inspire all who hear it to redouble their voices in praise of the Holy Trinity: Father, Son and Holy Spirit, to whom be glory and praise for ever and ever. Amen.

An Instrumental Group and their Instruments

GRANT harmony, Lord, to all gathered here to praise your name. Let there be no discord among those who use their talents to your glory, but rather let their music-making be a joyful counterpoint to the voices of the angels in heaven who praise your glory without ceasing. We ask you to pour out your blessings ✠ on this family of yours, and on their instruments, that they may be true worshippers in a spirit of service to the praise of God and the devotion of our congregation. We ask this through Christ our Lord. Amen.

Blessing of a Choir

SEE P. 215

FLAGS AND BANNERS

A National Flag

ALMIGHTY Father, whose reign is eternal, and whose kingdom has no end, source of all authority, we ask you to bless ✠ this symbol of our earthly nation, and grant to our country protection in time of need, prosperity for all and harmony between all. Grant us all a spirit of proper patriotism and love of our homeland that this flag may come to be respected throughout the world as a symbol of all that is virtuous, honourable and true, and may those who honour it today be found one day to be citizens of your heavenly kingdom, where you live and reign for ever and ever. Amen.

A Military Flag

LORD God of hosts, we pray your almighty blessing on this (regiment) and on this standard. May this flag symbolize all that is good, noble and true; all that is worth fighting for and defending. May its sight inspire us to great deeds in your service and in defence of our homeland; may it bring forth courage, steadfastness, clear reason, a sense of proportion, and justice. May it give us new strength when we are weary, confidence when we are unsure, and hope when all seems lost. And so may our nation go from strength to strength and build on this earth a kingdom fit for you and for all humankind. Through Christ our Lord. Amen.

May this flag and those who honour it be blessed in the name of the Father, and of the Son, ✠ and of the Holy Spirit. Amen.

A Processional Cross

LORD God Almighty, who led your faithful people through the desert towards the promised land by a pillar of fire, bless ✠, we pray, this standard of the cross, that we may follow the sign of your passion towards the promised land of heaven. Bless it as you blessed the bronze serpent which Moses caused to be lifted up on a spear in the desert, thus prefiguring the lifting up of your only begotten Son on the cross, and grant that we who look upon this cross may be healed from all infirmity of body and soul, and thus enabled to merit the salvation he won for us. Through the same Jesus Christ our Lord. Amen.

A Scout or Guide Flag
ALSO, OF COURSE, CUBS, BROWNIES, BEAVERS AND RAINBOWS

ALMIGHTY Father, who have used the scouting/guiding movement to the benefit of many young people, we ask your blessing ✠ on this (troop) and its flag. May they always strive to 'be prepared' to do their duty to you and this country, to help other people and to keep the scout/guide law. May the inspiration of Robert Baden Powell remain fresh in these young minds, that they may grow up to be worthy citizens of this land and of the kingdom of heaven. Through Christ our Lord. Amen.

A Church Banner

℣. Our help is in the name of the Lord.
℟. **Who made heaven and earth.**
℣. The Lord be with you.
℟. **And with your spirit.**

LORD Jesus Christ, whose Church is likened to an army with banners, bless ✠, we pray, this banner, that all who campaign for our Lord God may (through the intercession of Saint N.) overcome all our enemies in this life, whether visible or invisible, and after our victory is won, merit eternal triumph in heaven, where you live and reign for ever and ever. Amen.

RINGS

An Engagement Ring

ALMIGHTY God, without beginning or end, bless ✠, we pray, this ring, sign of endless love, and grant that he/she who wears it may be true to the one who loves him/her and to the covenant for which they have committed to prepare in the name of the Lord Jesus, who lives and reigns for ever and ever. Amen.

A Wedding Ring

The proper place for blessing a wedding ring is in the rite of marriage itself. However, it happens that replacements for wedding rings are sometimes necessary. A pastor may find this an appropriate occasion to encourage the couple concerned to renew their wedding vows. After this, the priest blesses the couple and their ring:

Let us pray.

LOOK down, O Lord, from heaven, and grant to your faithful children an increase of the grace you granted them on their wedding day. May they continue to be faithful in marriage, loving you, each other, (their children) and their neighbour as you command us, and may their love be a true reflection of the love of Father, Son and Holy Spirit. Amen.

MAY you be blessed ✠ by the same Holy Trinity, and may the Lord bless ✠ this ring which you give as a renewed sign of your love and fidelity in the name of the Father, and of the Son, and of the Holy Spirit. Amen.

A Claddagh Ring

AS you give your heart into your beloved's hands may your love be strengthened day by day; may the nine choirs of angels who sing God's praises keep you; may St Patrick and St Brigid pray for you, and may you one day come to see our Lord's own Sacred Heart in heaven. Through Christ our Lord. Amen.

M AY this claddagh ring be blessed in the name of the most holy Trinity: Father, Son ✠ and Holy Spirit. Amen.

A Signet Ring

B LESSED Lord, to whose family we were joined on the day of our baptism, bless ✠, we pray, this signet ring, sign of our family here on earth. May our loyalty to both our earthly and heavenly families be strengthened and supported by your grace, the prayers of the saints, and the love of those to whom we are bound by blood and affection. Through Christ our Lord. Amen.

A Rosary Ring
SEE ROSARIES, P. 21

ENGAGED COUPLES

෴ ⚜ ෴

BLESSING OF SEVERAL COUPLES
AT, FOR INSTANCE, A MARRIAGE PREPARATION DAY

There is a large selection of suitable readings in the Marriage section of the Lectionary.

A reading from the book of Tobit. 8:4–8

AS they prepared for their marriage, Tobias said to Sarah: 'Arise, and let us pray to the Lord that he may have mercy upon us.' And Tobias began to pray:

'You are blessed, O God of our Fathers; blessed be your holy and glorious name for ever. May heaven and all that you have made bless you. You created Adam and gave to him Eve his wife as help and support; and from them has descended the human race.

'For you said, "It is not good that man should be alone; let us make for him a helper that is like him." And now, Lord, I take this relative of mine not from lust, but in sincerity. Have mercy on us, and may we grow old together.' And together they said 'Amen.'

This is another version, (from the Vulgate), which differs. It should, perhaps, be pointed out that though Tobias refers to Sara as his sister, she is in fact his cousin.

AS they prepared for their marriage, Tobias said to Sara: 'Arise, and let us pray to God today and tomorrow, and the next day: because for these three nights we are joined to God: and when the third night is over, we will be in our own wedlock. For we are the children of saints, and we must not be joined together like heathens that do not know God.' So they both arose, and prayed earnestly together that health might be given them.

And Tobias said: 'Lord God of our fathers, may the heavens and the earth, and the sea, and the fountains, and the rivers, and all you creatures that are in them, bless you. You made Adam from the dust of the earth, and gave him Eve for a support; and now, Lord, you know that not for fleshly lust do I take my sister to wife, but only for the love of posterity, by which your name may be blessed for ever and ever.'

Sara also said: 'Have mercy on us, O Lord, have mercy on us, and let us both grow old together in health.'

Let us pray.

L ORD, strengthen the love and dedication of these couples who are preparing to celebrate the sacrament of marriage. Help them to see beyond their wedding day to the covenant that will endure until death. In this blessed time of engagement, may each come to know their betrothed better, that the love which they share may bear fruit in a happy marriage and ultimately eternal life in heaven. We ask this through Christ our Lord. Amen.

May almighty God bless you and keep you in his love: Father, Son ✠ and Holy Spirit. Amen.

Engagement rings may be blessed: see p. 58

An Individual Engaged Couple

G OD has established the holy Sacrament of Matrimony both for the increase of the human family, reborn in holy Baptism, for the mutual support and love of each other, and also as a sign of Christ's love for his Church. As you continue along the path to celebrate this great sacrament:

N. and N.: May God the Father of wisdom strengthen your knowledge of each other; may Christ our Lord who died for us teach you the meaning of true love; may the Holy Spirit be poured out upon you to fill you with his gifts and fruits in abundance.

And may almighty God bless you: the Father, and the Son, ✠ and the Holy Spirit. Amen.

AN EXPECTANT MOTHER
ESPECIALLY WHERE THERE ARE COMPLICATIONS

☙ ⚓ ❧

ANCIENT FORM

℣. Our help is in the name of the Lord.
℟. Who made heaven and earth.
℣. Lord, save your servant.
℟. Who has placed her trust in you, O God.
℣. Be to her, Lord, a tower of strength.
℟. In the face of the enemy.
℣. May the enemy be powerless against her.
℟. May the son of iniquity be unable to hurt her.
℣. Send her help, O Lord, from your holy place.
℟. And protect her out of Sion.
℣. O Lord, hear my prayer.
℟. And let my cry come to you.
℣. The Lord be with you.
℟. And with your spirit.

Let us pray.

ALMIGHTY, eternal God, who have given to your servants to acknowledge the true faith in the glory of the eternal Trinity, and to adore you as one God in powerful majesty, we pray that the strength of this faith may fortify your servant N. in her pregnancy. Through Christ our Lord. Amen.

LORD God, creator of all, strong and terrible yet just and merciful, who alone are truly good and loving, who freed Israel from every evil, making our forefathers your beloved, and who sanctified them with the hand of your Spirit; who prepared the body and soul of the glorious virgin Mary to be a fitting habitation for you; who filled John the Baptist with the Holy Spirit and caused him to leap for joy in the womb: Receive the sacrifice of a contrite spirit and the earnest desire of your servant N. that her unborn child whom you have given her may be kept from harm. Protect, O Lord, your own creation, and keep it safe from any harm that evil can do; be yourself the heavenly and merciful midwife who will bring her child to see the light of day, then grow and flourish, that together they may serve you and come to merit eternal life. Through Christ our Lord. Amen.

May the blessing of almighty God, Father, Son ✠ and Holy Spirit, come down on you and your child, and remain with you for ever. Amen.

ANOTHER BLESSING

A reading from the holy Gospel according to Luke.   1:26–38

IN the sixth month, the angel Gabriel was sent from God to a city of Galilee, called Nazareth, to a virgin espoused to a man whose name was Joseph, of the house of David: and the virgin's name was Mary. And the angel came in and said to her: Hail, full of grace, the Lord is with you: blessed are you among women. She, hearing this, was troubled at his saying and wondered to herself what manner of greeting this could be. And the angel said to her: Fear not, Mary, for you have found grace with God. Behold, you shall conceive in your womb and bring forth a son: and you shall call his name Jesus. He shall be great and shall be called the Son of the Most High. And the Lord God shall give him the throne of David his father: and he shall reign in the house of Jacob for ever. And of his kingdom there shall be no end. And Mary said to the angel: How shall this be done, because I am a virgin? And the angel said to her: The Holy Spirit shall come upon you and the power of the Most High shall overshadow you, and therefore too the child which shall be born shall be called Holy, the Son of God. And, behold, your cousin Elizabeth also has conceived a son in her old age: and she who was called barren is now in her sixth month, because nothing is impossible for God. And Mary said: Behold the handmaid of the Lord: be it done to me according to your word. And the angel departed from her.

HEAVENLY Father, and source of all life, we pray for this mother (N.) and her unborn child. Keep them both safe and well through pregnancy, and when the time comes for this child to be born into this world, grant them a speedy and easy labour. May this child be born healthy and strong, and be soon reborn in the waters of Baptism that it may speedily join your holy people in praising you, and come one day to the glory of heaven, where you live and reign for ever and ever. Amen.

May this unborn child and its mother be blessed in the name of the Father, and of the Son, ✠ and of the Holy Spirit. Amen.

BLESSING OF PARENTS AFTER CHILDBIRTH
WITH THE FIRST BRINGING OF THE CHILD TO CHURCH

❧ ✠ ❧

The parents may be met at the church door with the child, if this seems suitable. Otherwise, this rite could take place during the Mass at some suitable juncture.

℣. Our help is in the name of the Lord.
℟. **Who made heaven and earth.**

Addressing the child, the priest says:
N., welcome to the temple of God.

And to the parents, he says:
N. and N., let us together adore the Son of the Virgin Mary who has blessed you with a child/children.

If at the church door, all then proceed to the sanctuary step, where they kneel.

℣. O Lord hear my prayer.
℟. **And let my cry come to you.**
℣. The Lord be with you.
℟. **And with your spirit.**

Let us pray.

ALMIGHTY, eternal God, who, in sending your Son through the Blessed Virgin Mary has changed our mourning into dancing, look kindly, we beg, on your son and daughter who have come to church today to give you thanks for the safe delivery of their child N. Through the prayers of the same Virgin Mary, grant that they, together with their child, may come to the fullness of happiness in heaven. Through Christ our Lord. Amen.

And may the peace and blessing of Almighty God, Father, Son ✠ and Holy Spirit, come down upon you and your child, and remain with you for ever.

ANOTHER BLESSING OF A NEWBORN CHILD

A reading from the holy Gospel according to Luke.   2:21–32, 39, 40

AFTER eight days, when it was time that the child should be circumcised, his name was called Jesus, which he was called by the angel before he was conceived in the womb. And after the days of Mary's purification according to the law of Moses were accomplished, they carried him to Jerusalem, to present him to the Lord (for it is written in the law of the Lord: Every male who opens the womb shall be called holy to the Lord) and to offer in sacrifice, as it is written in the law of the Lord, a pair of turtledoves or two young pigeons.

And behold there was a man in Jerusalem named Simeon: and this man was just and devout, waiting for the consolation of Israel. And the Holy Spirit was in him. He had received a revelation from the Holy Spirit, that he should not see death before he had seen the Christ of the Lord. So inspired by the Spirit he came into the temple. And when his parents brought in the child Jesus, to do for him according to the custom of the law, he also took him into his arms and blessed God and said:

Now dismiss your servant in peace, O Lord, according to your word: Because my eyes have seen your salvation, which you have prepared before the face of all peoples: A light for revelation to the Gentiles and the glory of your people Israel.

After they had performed all things according to the law of the Lord, they returned to Galilee, to their city, Nazareth. And the child grew and became strong, full of wisdom: and the grace of God was in him.

HEAVENLY Father, we give you thanks for the safe birth of this child, and for the joy you have given to his/her parents. Your holy Church rejoices too, that one more soul has been entrusted to her hands, and we pray that this child may, like your Son, grow strong, be full of wisdom and grace. We thank you also that the time of pregnancy and birth is now over, and we ask your blessing on the joyful months and years ahead. May N. and N. be good parents to this child; grant them your gifts of patience, tolerance, firmness, wisdom and good humour, that they, together with this newborn child may one day come to praise you in heaven, where you live and reign for ever and ever. Amen.

May these parents and their child be blessed by Almighty God, the Father, the Son ✠ and the Holy Spirit. Amen.

MARRIAGE

⚜

A WEDDING ANNIVERSARY

Psalm 116 (117)

PRAISE the Lord, all you nations,
acclaim him all you peoples,
For his love has been confirmed upon us
and the faithfulness of the Lord shall abide for ever.
Glory be to the Father and to the Son
and to the Holy Spirit,
As it was in the beginning, is now and ever shall be,
world without end. Amen.

℣. Send them help, O Lord, from your holy place.
℟. **And protect them out of Sion.**

℣. O Lord, hear my prayer.
℟. **And let my cry come to you.**

℣. The Lord be with you.
℟. **And with your spirit.**

Let us pray.

SEND forth, O Lord, your right hand of help to these your faithful people that they may always seek you with all their hearts, and may always deserve to receive what they rightly ask from you.

ALMIGHTY eternal God, look kindly on these your rejoicing serv-ants who give thanks today for N. years of marriage. Grant that they may always trust in you alone, and know the abundant riches of your grace; may they continue ever one in love, and after the journey of this life is over, may they (together with their children) deserve to come to the blessedness of eternal joy. Through Christ our Lord. Amen.

May the blessing of almighty God, Father, Son ✠ and Holy Spirit, come down on you and remain with you for ever. Amen.

A Married Couple

ALMIGHTY God, whose Son not only honoured a marriage feast with his presence, but began there his wonderful ministry of miracles, be pleased to bless ✠ these your servants N. and N. Grant them harmony, lasting love, affectionate restraint, and a humble respect for each other. Give them a true appreciation of your holy laws and the great dignity of a profound faith. May your holy angel be their constant guardian. Free them from all temptation to sin. May their days be long and full of peace [and their children their joy], that both on earth and in heaven, the joy of God himself may be their crown. Through the same Christ our Lord. Amen.

Blessing of a New Wedding Ring
SEE P. 58

WORKPLACES

❧ ✟ ❧

An Office

A reading from the holy Gospel according to Matthew.   9:9

JESUS saw a man sitting in the tax office, named Matthew; and he said to him: Follow me. And he rose up and followed him.

Let us pray.

ALMIGHTY God, who in creating the world laboured fruitfully six days and rested on the seventh, we pray that you bless ✟ this office and all those who work here. May all that happens in this place be also fruitful, and fulfil what it sets out to do with efficiency and also with a due regard to ethics and the charity that is due to our neighbour. May there be also respect, liking and good relations between those who work here; may those in charge never expect too much from those whom they employ, and may employees behave responsibly and honestly towards those under whom they work. Dear Lord, may this office become part of your Kingdom, for your glory and the good of humanity. Through Jesus Christ our Lord. Amen.

Should a lighter touch be required, the following could be added:

Lord, may this office become a branch office of your Kingdom, and may we take all our more important orders directly from you. Amen.

A Computer System

HEAVENLY Father, the source of all that is good, whose Word has gone forth to the utmost bounds of the world, we ask your blessing ✟ on this computer/server/media installation and on all those who will use it. May it be an inspiration to do good, a profitable investment and at the same time further your kingdom, where you live and reign for ever and ever. Amen.

A Personal Computer

Lord Jesus Christ, the Word and the Wisdom of God, we pray your blessing ✠ on this computer and on N. who will use it. Grant us discretion and the will to do as you command in our use of this machine, that it may further both the love of you and the service of our neighbour, who live and reign for ever and ever. Amen.

Prayer before using the internet: see p. 148

A Workshop

L ORD Jesus Christ, who were content to be known as a carpenter for most of your life on earth, we pray that you bless ✠ this workshop. May those who work here find joy in the labour of their hands, and as they work, raise their minds to you, the maker of all that is, the divine Craftsman who made the world. May there be always harmony and good cheer, and also a healthy profit in this establishment, that all who work here, and all who bring their custom here, may one day be united in heaven with your Father and the Holy Spirit, who live and reign for ever and ever. Amen.

A Shop

L ORD Jesus Christ, who likened the Kingdom of God to a merchant finding a pearl of great price, we ask you to bless ✠ this shop and all who work here. May this business flourish and be profitable; may it bring happiness to those who live in this area, and satisfaction to those who work here. In its own way, may it contribute to the building up of your kingdom where you live and reign for ever and ever. Amen.

A Farm

A farm would be best blessed with the Rogationtide procession in the days immediately preceding Ascension day. See p. 203. Otherwise, the following is suggested.

A reading from the book of Genesis. 1:11–12

G OD said: let the earth bring forth vegetation, and such plants that bear seed, and the fruit tree yielding fruit after its kind, which may have seed in itself upon the earth. And it was so done. And the earth brought forth vegetation, and such things that bear seed according to its kind, and the tree that bears fruit, having seed according to its kind. And God saw that it was good.

A reading from the book of Psalms.   64:10–14 (65:9–13)

YOU have visited the earth, and plentifully watered it; you have in many ways enriched it.

The river of God is filled with water, you have prepared their food: for so is its preparation.

You fill up its furrows plentifully and multiply its fruits; it shall grow up and rejoice in its showers.

You will crown the year with your goodness: and your fields shall be filled with plenty.

The beautiful places of the wilderness shall grow lush, and the hills shall be girded about with joy,

The rams of the flock are clothed, and the vales shall abound with corn: they shall shout, yes they shall sing a hymn of joy.

Let us pray.

LORD God, who have commanded that we the human race should labour with our hands for what we eat, we ask you to bless ✠ these fields and those who work here. May this land yield not just a living for those who work here, but also much joy as they participate year by year in your wonderful work of creation and see under their own hands your own creative power. May the beasts be content and the crops bountiful, and both free from disease or any pestilence, that all may rejoice in you, the maker and preserver of all, who live and reign for ever and ever. Amen.

SEAS AND RIVERS

BLESSING OF THE SEA

Some or all of this litany can be used in procession towards the sea.

PROCESSIONAL LITANY

Lord, have mercy,	**Lord, have mercy.**
Christ, have mercy,	**Christ, have mercy.**
Lord, have mercy,	**Lord, have mercy.**
God the almighty Father,	**have mercy on us.**
God the Son, Redeemer of the world,	**have mercy on us.**
God the Holy Spirit,	**have mercy on us.**
Holy Trinity, one God,	**have mercy on us.**
O God, whose Spirit hovered over the deep,	**have mercy on us.**
O God, who divided the waters on the first day,	**have mercy on us.**
O God, who created the land and the sea on the second day,	**have mercy on us.**
O God, who made the creatures of the sea on the fifth day,	**have mercy on us.**
O God, who caused four rivers to flow out of Eden,	**have mercy on us.**
O God, who rescued Noah and his family from the mighty flood,	**have mercy on us.**
O God, who promised that never again shall a flood destroy the earth,	**have mercy on us.**
O God, who caused that the infant Moses should be rescued from the waters,	**have mercy on us.**
O God, who turned the waters of the Nile into blood,	**have mercy on us.**
O God, who parted the waters of the sea for the Children of Israel,	**have mercy on us.**

O God, who made sweet the
    bitter waters in the desert, **have mercy on us.**

O God, who gave water
    from the rock at Meribah, **have mercy on us.**

O God, who commanded the use of water
    for the solemn rites of purification, **have mercy on us.**

O God, who caused the Israelites to cross
    the waters of the Jordan to enter the
    promised land dry-shod, **have mercy on us.**

O God, who caused Zadok and Nathan
    to anoint Solomon at the
    spring of Gihon, **have mercy on us.**

O God, who parted the waters
    for Elijah and Elisha, **have mercy on us.**

O God, who purified with salt
    the waters for Elisha, **have mercy on us.**

O God, who saved your servant
    Jonah from the mighty waters, **have mercy on us.**

O God, whose voice thunders
    over the immensity of waters, **have mercy on us.**

O God, who store up the
    depths of the sea, **have mercy on us.**

O God, who visit the earth
    and give it water, **have mercy on us.**

O God, who rescue your servants from the
    mire and from the mighty waters, **have mercy on us.**

O God, who make the waters
    higher than a mountain, **have mercy on us.**

O God, who measure the waters
    in the hollow of your hand, **have mercy on us.**

O God, who hold us as we pass
    through raging waters so that
    we are not overwhelmed, **have mercy on us.**

O God, who called John
    to baptize in water, **have mercy on us.**

O God, whose Son was baptized by John in the waters of the Jordan,	**have mercy on us.**
O God, who promised living water to the woman of Samaria,	**have mercy on us.**
O God, who established Baptism as the Sacrament of Regeneration,	**have mercy on us.**
O God, whose Son calmed the storms on the Sea of Galilee,	**have mercy on us.**
O God, whose Son walked upon the raging waters,	**have mercy on us.**
O God, who rescued St Paul from shipwreck and drowning,	**have mercy on us.**
Jesus, Son of the Living God,	**have mercy on us.**
Holy Mary, Mother of God,	**pray for us.**
Holy Virgin of Virgins,	**pray for us.**
Holy Mary, Star of the Sea,	**pray for us.**
St Peter and St Andrew, Fishermen,	**pray for us.**
St Brendan the Navigator,	**pray for us.**
St Francis of Paola, Patron of Sailors,	**pray for us.**
St Clare of Assisi, Patron of good weather,	**pray for us.**
St Elmo,	**pray for us.**
St Benno,	**pray for us.**
St Christopher, patron of travellers,	**pray for us.**
St Clement,	**pray for us.**
St Elizabeth Seton,	**pray for us.**
St Julian,	**pray for us.**
St Nicholas,	**pray for us.**
St Albinus,	**pray for us.**
St Castulus,	**pray for us.**
St Florian,	**pray for us.**
St Hyacinth,	**pray for us.**
St Maximin,	**pray for us.**
St Michael,	**pray for us.**

St Wulfram,	**pray for us.**
(Local saints)	**pray for us.**
All holy men and women,	**pray for us.**
That you would guide and protect your Holy Church,	**Lord, we ask you, hear our prayer.**
That you would preserve in safety all fisherfolk,	**Lord, we ask you, hear our prayer.**
That you would conserve and multiply the fish you give us for our food,	**Lord, we ask you, hear our prayer.**
That you would bring to safety all migrants and travellers,	**Lord, we ask you, hear our prayer.**
That you would protect all seafarers from piracy,	**Lord, we ask you, hear our prayer.**
That you would comfort and protect coastguards and lighthouse workers,	**Lord, we ask you, hear our prayer.**
That you would keep swimmers and surfers in safety,	**Lord, we ask you, hear our prayer.**
That you would fortify and protect lifeguards and lifeboatmen,	**Lord, we ask you, hear our prayer.**
That you would protect and make skilful those who work in air-sea rescue,	**Lord, we ask you, hear our prayer.**
That you would comfort with your presence those who work on cruise ships,	**Lord, we ask you, hear our prayer.**
That you would comfort with your presence those who work on tankers and container ships,	**Lord, we ask you, hear our prayer.**
That you would foster the conservation and protection of our seas,	**Lord, we ask you, hear our prayer.**

That you would protect us
from floods, from typhoons
and from storms, **Lord, we ask you, hear our prayer.**

That you would protect us from
extreme weather of every kind, **Lord, we ask you, hear our prayer.**

Christ, hear us. **Christ, hear us.**

Lord Jesus, hear our prayer. **Lord Jesus, hear our prayer.**

Let us pray.

ALMIGHTY ever-living God, Father of transcendent majesty, whose invisible power is manifest in your visible creation; whose Spirit brooded over the waters at the beginning of the world, grant to us, your servants, that as often as we see with our bodily eyes the mighty waters rising in great waves below the sky, we may be enraptured in contemplation of your hidden mysteries. May such a sight and the thoughts it arouses prompt us to call upon your holy name and glorify it, and, since all creation is under your sway, to give you the homage of our hearts in true humility and devotion. Through Christ our Lord. Amen.

LORD Jesus Christ, who walked upon the waters, who commanded the raging tempest of wind and sea to be calm; have mercy on us, your servants, surrounded by so many perils of this life; and grant that by the power of your blessing ✠ on these waters all malicious spirits may be driven away, dangerous tempests may subside, and through the intercession of the Immaculate Virgin, your Mother, that all who sail on these seas may safely reach their destination, and at last return secure to their homes. Who live and reign for ever and ever. Amen.

O LORD, who said: 'By the sweat of your brow you must eat your bread'; mercifully listen to our prayers and grant your blessing ✠ on this sea, so that all who must earn their daily bread for themselves and their families on these waters may be enriched with your bounty and offer you due thanks for your generosity. Through Christ our Lord. Amen.

Holy water

A Fishing Boat

A reading from the holy Gospel according to John.   21:1–14

AFTER [his resurrection,] Jesus showed himself again to the disciples at the sea of Tiberias. And he showed himself in this manner. There were Simon Peter, and Thomas, who is called Didymus, and Nathanael, who was from Cana of Galilee, and the sons of Zebedee, and two others of his disciples. Simon Peter said to them: 'I will go fishing.' They say to him: 'We will also come.' And they went out, and got into the boat: and that night they caught nothing. But when the morning had come, Jesus stood on the shore, yet the disciples did not know that it was Jesus. Jesus therefore said to them: 'Children, have you any fish?' They answered him: 'No.' He said to them: 'Cast the net on the right side of the ship, and you shall find some.' So they cast their net; and now they were not able to draw it in for the multitude of fishes. That disciple therefore whom Jesus loved, said to Peter: 'It is the Lord.' Simon Peter, when he heard that it was the Lord, wrapped his cloak about him, (for he was naked,) and cast himself into the sea. But the other disciples came in the ship, (for they were not far from land, but about two hundred cubits,) dragging the net with the fish. As soon then as they came to land, they saw hot coals lying with fish laid on them, and bread. Jesus said to them: 'Bring some of the fish which you have just caught.' Simon Peter went up and drew the net to land, full of great fish, one hundred and fifty-three. And although there were so many, the net was not broken. Jesus said to them: 'Come, and eat.' And none of them who were at the meal dared ask him: 'Who are you?' knowing that it was the Lord. And Jesus came and took bread, and gave it to them, and gave them fish in the same way. This was now the third time that Jesus showed himself to his disciples after he had risen from the dead.

LORD Jesus Christ, friend of fishermen, who calmed the storm on the sea of Galilee, and granted a miraculous draught of fishes to your disciples, we ask the same blessings on this boat and its crew. May this boat [or The N.] remain safe to the end of its working days, and may those who work on board be likewise under your powerful protection. And may this boat find plentiful fish and a good profit. Who live and reign for ever and ever. Amen.

May this boat and all who work in her be blessed by the Father, the Son ✠ and the Holy Spirit. Amen.

A reading from the holy Gospel according to Matthew.   5:1–10

SEEING the multitudes, Jesus went up onto a mountain, and when he had sat down, his disciples came to him, and opening his mouth he taught them, saying:

Blessed are the poor in spirit: for theirs is the kingdom of heaven.

Blessed are the meek: for they shall possess the land.

Blessed are those who mourn: for they shall be comforted.

Blessed are those who hunger and thirst after justice: for they shall have their fill.

Blessed are the merciful: for they shall obtain mercy.

Blessed are the pure of heart: they shall see God.

Blessed are the peacemakers: for they shall be called the children of God.

Blessed are those who suffer persecution for justice' sake: for theirs is the kingdom of heaven.

LORD God of hosts, whose arm is mighty and whose ways are peace, we ask your blessing ✠ on this ship N. and on all who sail in her. In particular, we dedicate this ship to the preservation of peace, and we pray that it may never have to fire a shot in anger, nor suffer attack from a hostile enemy. May those who serve here do their duty by their country and also by you their Creator and Preserver, who live and reign for ever and ever. Amen.

Blessing of a Boat or Ship before a Voyage

℣. Our help is in the name of the Lord.
℟. **Who made heaven and earth.**

℣. The Lord be with you.
℟. **And with your spirit.**

Let us pray.

LISTEN kindly to our prayers, O Father, and as you sent your blessing on the ark of Noah as it was borne over the flood, with your holy right hand bless ✠ this boat and all who will sail in her. Stretch out your hand to them, as you did to Peter when he walked upon the sea, and send your holy angel from heaven to keep the boat and all in it from every harm. Keep them safe, grant them a tranquil voyage and a safe harbour; and once their journey is done, bring them home content. Through Christ our Lord. Amen.

A Ship

A reading from the holy Gospel according to Luke. 8:22–25

IT came to pass on a certain day that Jesus went into a little ship with his disciples. And he said to them: Let us go over to the other side of the lake. And they launched forth. And when they were sailing, he slept. And there came down a storm of wind upon the lake: and they were filled with water and were in danger. And they came and awakened him, saying: 'Master, we perish.' But he, arising, rebuked the wind and the rage of the water, whereupon it ceased, and there was a calm. And he said to them: 'Where is your faith?' They, being afraid, wondered, saying one to the other: 'Who is this that commands both the winds and the sea, and they obey him?'

HEAR our prayers, Lord and master of the waves, for this ship, N., which we bless in the name of the Father, the Son ✠ and the Holy Spirit. May all, officers, crew and passengers, travel safely in her, may all who earn their living by means of her prosper, and by faith working in love, may we all come one day from the storms of this world to the port of eternal bliss. Through Christ our Lord. Amen.

A Lifeboat

A reading from the holy Gospel according to Luke. 8:22–25

IT came to pass on a certain day that Jesus went into a little ship with his disciples. And he said to them: Let us go over to the other side of the lake. And they launched forth. And when they were sailing, he slept. And there came down a storm of wind upon the lake: and they were filled with water and were in danger. And they came and awakened him, saying: 'Master, we perish.' But he, arising, rebuked the wind and the rage of the water, whereupon it ceased, and there was a calm. And he said to them: 'Where is your faith?' They, being afraid, wondered, saying one to the other: 'Who is this that commands both the winds and the sea, and they obey him?'

LORD Jesus Christ, master of the deep, whom the winds and the sea obey, we ask you to keep this lifeboat and all who shall work in it safe in your loving care. May none be lost who are in need of this boat's assistance, and as you rescued St Peter as you walked upon the waves, so aid with your powerful help those who seek to pull others from the waters, that all may one day recognize you as their true Saviour and come to the port of eternal bliss. Who live and reign for ever and ever. Amen.

May this lifeboat, and all who work in it be blessed by the Father, the Son ✠ and the Holy Spirit. Amen.

In Danger of Flood

℣. Come to our help, O God our Saviour!
℟. **Deliver us for your name's sake!**

℣. O Lord, save your servants!
℟. **Who place all their trust in you.**

℣. Do not treat us as our sins deserve, Lord.
℟. **Nor punish us for our transgressions.**

℣. Lord, help us from your holy place.
℟. **And watch over us from Sion.**

℣. O Lord, hear my prayer.
℟. **And let my cry come to you.**

℣. The Lord be with you.
℟. **And with your spirit.**

Let us pray.

O GOD, giver of saving grace even to the wicked, and who desire not the death of the sinner, humbly we call on you in your glory, begging that you protect with your heavenly assistance your servants who put their trust in you from all dangers of flood. May they find in you a steadfast protector, so that they may always serve you and that no fear or temptation separate them from you. Through Christ our Lord. Amen.

May the blessing of almighty God, Father, Son ✠ and Holy Spirit, come upon these waters and keep them always in their bounds. Amen.

and/or

O LORD, who walk upon the wings of the winds, who walked upon the waters of Galilee and who calmed the raging of those same waters, help us, lest we perish! Calm the inundation that threatens us; strengthen the banks that restrain the mighty waters. Keep us in safety, God of thunders, that we may give you joyful thanks for all your goodness. Through Christ our Lord. Amen.

Blessing of a Bridge

℣. Our help is in the name of the Lord.
℟. **Who made heaven and earth.**
℣. The Lord be with you.
℟. **And with your spirit.**

Let us pray.

L ORD, hear our prayers, and be pleased to bless ✠ this bridge and all who pass over it, that they may ever find in you a protector and support amidst the joys and sorrows of this changing world. Through Christ our Lord. Amen.

H OLY Lord and Father, almighty everlasting God, hear our prayer, and in your goodness send your holy angel from heaven to watch over, protect, and support this bridge and all who cross on it. Through Christ our Lord. Amen.

Holy water

VEHICLES

A Car
TRADITIONAL BLESSING

℣. Our help is in the name of the Lord.
℟. Who made heaven and earth.
℣. The Lord be with you.
℟. And with your spirit.

Let us pray.

HEAR our prayers, O Lord, and bless ✠ this vehicle with your powerful hand; send your holy angels to accompany it, to protect all who travel in it from harm. And as by the hand of your Apostle Philip you gave faith and grace to the Ethiopian who read your holy word in his chariot, so show your faithful servants who use this vehicle the way of salvation. May they, helped by your grace, become strong in good works and be found worthy to enter eternal life when the many chances of life's journey are done. Through Christ our Lord. Amen.

Another Blessing for a Car

HEAVENLY Father, we ask you to bless ✠ this car and keep all who travel in it safe from harm. May they journey with due regard to safety and the law of the land, but also to the greater law of charity to our neighbour. And as you sent your angel Raphael to watch over Tobias on his journey, so send your angel to watch over this car and all who use it. Through Christ our Lord. Amen.

A Van or Lorry

℣. Our help is in the name of the Lord.
℟. Who made heaven and earth.
℣. The Lord be with you.
℟. And with your spirit.

Let us pray.

ALMIGHTY God, who commanded that we should earn our bread by the sweat of our brow, bless ✠, we pray, this van/lorry, dedicated to that end. Guide our hands and our hearts to patient and charitable road use, and may all our work tend not only to our health in this life, but to our eternal salvation. Through Christ our Lord. Amen.

A Military Vehicle

℣. Our help is in the name of the Lord.
℟. Who made heaven and earth.
℣. The Lord be with you.
℟. And with your spirit.

Let us pray.

ALL-CONQUERING God, whose ways are peace, we ask your blessing ✠ on this N. We pray that it may be effective to protect and defend the vulnerable and defenceless, and thus play its part in the building up of your kingdom. May those who travel in it be kept safe from all harm, and strive to do good at all times. Through Jesus Christ our Lord. Amen.

An Aeroplane

A reading from the book of Ecclesiasticus.   43:10–18, 29–33

THE glory of the stars is the beauty of heaven; the Lord enlightens the world on high. By the words of the holy one they stand as he decrees, and shall never fail as they watch. Look upon the rainbow, and bless him that made it: it is very beautiful in its brightness; it encompasses the heavens with the circle of its glory, the hands of the most High have displayed it. By his commandment he makes the snow to fall fast, and sends forth swiftly the lightnings of his judgment. In the same way are his treasuries opened, and the clouds fly out like birds. By his greatness he has arranged the clouds, and shattered the hailstones. At the sight of him shall the mountains be shaken, and at his will the south wind shall blow. The noise of his thunder shall strike the earth, so too the northern storm, and the whirlwind.

We shall say much, and yet shall lack words: but the sum of our words is, He is all. What shall we be able to do to glorify him, for the Almighty himself is above all his works? The Lord is terrible, and exceedingly great, and his power is admirable. Glorify the Lord as much as ever you can, for he will yet far exceed you, and his magnificence is wonderful. Bless the Lord, exalt him as much as you can; for he is above all praise.

Let us pray.

LORD of the Universe, whose hands shaped the skies and caused the mighty winds to blow, and who gave intelligence to humanity to use these wonderful works of your creation to serve its needs, we pray for those who will work in or travel in this aircraft. May all come safely to their destinations, and finally to the port of eternal bliss, where you live and reign for ever and ever. Amen.

May this aircraft, and all who fly in her be blessed in the name of the Father, and of the Son, ✠ and of the Holy Spirit. Amen.

EMERGENCY VEHICLES

⚜

A Fire Engine

A reading from the second book of Samuel. 22:28–34

O GOD, you will save the poor, and with your eyes you will humble the haughty. For you are my lamp, O Lord, and you, O Lord, will enlighten my darkness. For in you I will run protected; in my God I will leap over the wall. Our God, his way is immaculate, the word of the Lord is tested by fire: he is the shield of all that trust in him. Who is God but the Lord: and who is strong but our God? God who has girded me with strength, and made my way perfect, making my feet like the feet of deer, and setting me upon the heights.

Let us pray.

A LMIGHTY God, who have created fire for the benefit of the human race, and who have chosen to appear to Moses in the burning bush and pillar of fire, and to our Lady and the Apostles in the form of countless tongues of fire, grant strength and protection to all who travel and use this engine for the saving of life and property. Guide their hands that they may be deft, and their feet that they may be sure in whatever perilous situation they may find themselves. Give them sure confidence in you, who are the merciful Creator and Restorer of humankind, who live and reign for ever and ever. Amen.

May this engine, and all who work with it be blessed in the name of the Father, and of the Son, ✠ and of the Holy Spirit. Amen.

An Ambulance

A reading from the holy Gospel according to Mark. 2:1–12

J ESUS entered into Capharnaum after some days, and it was heard that he was there in the house. And many people gathered, so that there was no room even at the door. And he spoke the word to them. And they came to him, bringing a paralytic, who was carried by four men. And when they could not bring him to him because of the crowd, they uncovered the roof where he was: and opening it, they let down the bed on which the paralytic lay. When Jesus had seen their faith, he said to the paralytic: 'Son, your sins are forgiven.' And there were some of the scribes sitting there and thinking in their hearts: 'Why does this man speak like this? He blasphemes. Who can forgive sins, but God?' Jesus immediately knowing in his spirit what they thought within themselves, said to them: 'Why are you thinking these things in your hearts? Which is easier; to say to the paralytic: your sins are forgiven, or to say: rise, take up your bed and walk? But so that you may know that the Son of man has power on earth to forgive sins'—he said to the paralytic—'I say to you: Rise; take up your bed and go home.' And immediately he arose and, taking up his bed, went his way in the sight of all: so that everyone wondered and glorified God, saying: 'We never saw anything like this.'

Let us pray.

LORD God, who have commanded us to care for the sick as a corporal work of mercy, we ask your blessing on this ambulance and all who will travel in it, the crew, and those who are sick. May it travel speedily, but in safety, and never fail to bring help to those who need it in their time of trial. We ask this through Christ our Lord. Amen.

May this ambulance, and all those who use it be blessed in the name of the Father, and of the Son, ✠ and of the Holy Spirit. Amen.

A LIFEBOAT

SEE P. 79

HORTICULTURE

Seeds

℣. Our help is in the name of the Lord.
℟. **Who made heaven and earth.**
℣. The Lord be with you.
℟. **And with your spirit.**

Let us pray.

A LMIGHTY God, who provide seed for the sowing and wine to cheer men's hearts, whose only-begotten Son lay buried in the earth to bring forth life: bless ✠, we pray, these seeds and bring them to life for our use, that our hearts may be cheered, and that we may reap a harvest of thanksgiving to your glory. Through Christ our Lord. Amen.

A Garden

A reading from the Song of Songs.   2:1–5
An allegory of the love of Christ and his Church for each other.

I AM the flower of the field, and the lily of the valley. As the lily among thorns, so is my love among daughters. As the apple tree among the trees of the woods, so is my beloved among sons. I sat down under his shadow, whom I desired: and his fruit was sweet to my taste. He brought me into his wine cellar, he filled me with love. Surround me with flowers, compass me about with apples: for I languish with love.

℣. Our help is in the name of the Lord.
℟. **Who made heaven and earth.**
℣. The Lord be with you.
℟. **And with your spirit.**

Let us pray.

ALMIGHTY God, who cause all things to grow and who delight in beauty and order, bless ✠ this small corner of your world; make it grow and prosper, to delight our hearts and feed us in body and soul. May we who seek you in your beautiful creation, while seeking, find and eventually come to that garden of Paradise where you live and reign for ever and ever. Amen.

AN ALLOTMENT

A reading from the book of Genesis. 3:17–19

WITH labour and toil shall you eat of the earth all the days of your life. Thorns and thistles shall it bring forth for you; and you shall eat the plants of the earth. With sweat on your face shall you eat bread till you return to the earth out of which you were taken: for dust you are, and unto dust you shall return.

℣. Our help is in the name of the Lord.
℟. **Who made heaven and earth.**
℣. The Lord be with you.
℟. **And with your spirit.**

Let us pray.

ALMIGHTY God, who make even a curse a blessing, and who commanded that we bring forth food from the earth by the sweat of our brow: bless ✠ this allotment, we pray, and grant that thorns and thistles may keep their distance, noxious flies flee; bugs, slugs and snails slither hence at the frown of your face, that the harvest may be plentiful and the recreation beneficial. Through Christ our Lord. Amen.

AN ORCHARD

A reading from the book of Leviticus. 26:3–5

IF you walk in my precepts, and keep my commandments, and put them into practice, I will give you rain in due season. And the ground shall bring forth its increase, and the trees shall be filled with fruit. The threshing of your harvest shall reach vintage, and the vintage shall last until the sowing time: and you shall eat your bread to the full, and dwell in your land without fear.

℣. Our help is in the name of the Lord.
℟. **Who made heaven and earth.**
℣. The Lord be with you.
℟. **And with your spirit.**

Let us pray.

ALMIGHTY God, who placed Adam and Eve in a garden of delights, full of trees of every kind, bless ✠ this orchard, and grant that we may both tend these trees faithfully and keep your commands, that we may reap a harvest of joy both in this life and in the eternal life to come. Through Christ our Lord. Amen.

A Vineyard

A reading from the book of Proverbs. 3:9–10

HONOUR the Lord with your substance, and give to him the first of all your fruits, so your barns shall be filled with abundance, and your presses shall run over with wine.

℣. Our help is in the name of the Lord.
℟. **Who made heaven and earth.**
℣. The Lord be with you.
℟. **And with your spirit.**

Let us pray.

ALMIGHTY God, who give us wine to cheer our hearts, and even chose the substance of wine to perpetuate your presence among us in the Eucharist: we pray that you bless ✠ this vineyard to your glory and our use. Keep far away all pestilence and foul weather, that the harvest may be plentiful and the vintage fine. Through God's new wine, Christ our Lord. Amen.

A Compost Heap

(NOT TO BE TAKEN ENTIRELY SERIOUSLY)

Let us pray.

ALMIGHTY God, who raised thy servant Job from the dunghill; and who from the same doth raise the poor of the land, and who looketh upon the lowly from thy glory; grant to this humble but useful corner of this (garden, farm) that it may steam away to thy glory and our use. Through Christ our Lord. Amen.

PART III

PRAYERS

For all sorts of people in all sorts of situations.

THE DYING

There are official rites for the Sacrament of Anointing of the Sick and Dying, also for the administration of Viaticum, the Sacrament of Penance and the Apostolic Indulgence; the prayers given in this book must not be considered a legitimate alternative. However, it often happens that, pastorally, one needs something else in addition, and although most rituals do provide prayers for these occasions, they are not always felt to be useful in every situation which presents itself to the pastor. In practice, these days most people are not conscious when death is near; therefore, once the sacraments have been administered to the person dying, prayers involving those assisting at the deathbed should predominate.

A Litany for the Dying

Roman Ritual, tr. John Henry Newman

Kýrie eléison.	**Kýrie eléison.**
Christe eléison.	**Christe eléison.**
Kýrie eléison.	**Kýrie eléison.**
Holy Mary,	**pray for him/her.**
All holy Angels,	**pray for him/her.**
Holy Abraham,	**pray for him/her.**
St John Baptist,	**pray for him/her.**
St Joseph,	**pray for him/her.**
St Peter,	**pray for him/her.**
St Paul,	**pray for him/her.**
St Andrew,	**pray for him/her.**
St John,	**pray for him/her.**
All Apostles,	**pray for him/her.**
All Evangelists,	**pray for him/her.**
All holy Disciples of the Lord,	**pray for him/her.**
All holy Innocents,	**pray for him/her.**
All holy Martyrs,	**pray for him/her.**

All holy Confessors,	**pray for him/her.**
All holy Hermits,	**pray for him/her.**
All holy Virgins,	**pray for him/her.**
All ye Saints of God,	**pray for him/her.**
Be merciful, be gracious,	**spare him/her, Lord.**
Be merciful, be gracious,	**Lord, deliver him/her.**
From the sins that are past,	**Lord, deliver him/her.**
From thy frown and thine ire,	**Lord, deliver him/her.**
From the perils of dying,	**Lord, deliver him/her.**
From any complying with sin,	**Lord, deliver him/her.**
Or denying his/her God,	**Lord, deliver him/her.**
Or relying on self at the last,	**Lord, deliver him/her.**
From the nethermost fire,	**Lord, deliver him/her.**
From all that is evil,	**Lord, deliver him/her.**
From power of the devil thy servant deliver,	**Lord, deliver him/her.**
For once and for ever.	**Lord, deliver him/her.**
By thy birth, and by thy Cross,	**Lord, deliver him/her.**
Rescue him/her from endless loss,	**Lord, deliver him/her.**
By thy death and burial,	**Lord, deliver him/her.**
Save him/her from a final fall,	**Lord, deliver him/her.**
By thy rising from the tomb,	**Lord, deliver him/her.**
By thy mounting up above,	**Lord, deliver him/her.**
By the Spirit's gracious love,	**Lord, deliver him/her.**
Save him/her in the day of doom.	**Lord, deliver him/her.**

Rescue him/her, O Lord,
   in this his/her evil hour,
      as of old so many by thy gracious power,
	Amen.

Enoch and Elijah from the common doom,	**Amen.**
Noah from the waters in a saving home,	**Amen.**
Abraham from th' abounding guilt of heathenness,	**Amen.**
Job from all his multiform and fell distress,	**Amen.**

Isaac, when his father's knife
    was raised to slay,   **Amen.**

Lot from burning Sodom
    on its judgement-day,   **Amen.**

Moses from the land
    of bondage and despair,   **Amen.**

Daniel from the hungry lions in their lair,   **Amen.**

And the children Three
    amid the furnace-flame,   **Amen.**

Chaste Susanna from the slander
    and the shame,   **Amen.**

David from Goliath and the wrath of Saul,   **Amen.**

And the two Apostles
    from their prison-thrall,   **Amen.**

Thecla from her torments,
    —so, to show thy power,
    rescue this thy servant in his/her final hour. **Amen.**

Brief Prayers for the Dying

It is said that hearing is the last sense to fail, and therefore a dying person is often able to benefit from some thoughts and prayers, even though unable to give any external sign. The priest can ask the person to give internal assent to prayers he makes in their name.

I firmly believe in the Christian, Catholic faith handed down to us from the apostles, and in the saving blood of our Lord Jesus Christ I place all my trust.

I hope most firmly in the salvation which our Lord Jesus Christ won for us in his passion, death and resurrection.

I love God, Father, Son and Holy Spirit, with all my heart, and for his sake I love my neighbour as myself.

I repent with all my heart that I have ever sinned, and I pray God to forgive me.

I accept my death and any pains that accompany it as just penance for my sins.

As I hope to be forgiven by God, I now freely forgive all those who have hurt me in this life, and I beg forgiveness of all those whom I have hurt.

I implore the saints and angels to watch over those whom I love on earth until we meet again.

I beg the saints, above all the Blessed Virgin Mary and my patron saints to pray for me now.

Into your hands I commend my spirit; Lord Jesus, receive my soul.

Jesus, mercy; Mary, help! Jesus, save me! Jesus, be a saviour to me! Mary, be a mother to me!

Lord Jesus Christ, Son of the living God, have mercy on me, a sinner.

Jesus, remember me when you come into your kingdom.

The following prayer is particularly useful in the case of those with an Irish background; it has often been prayed from infancy, and may be used as a way of indicating gently that death is near.

JESUS, Mary and Joseph, I give you my heart and my soul.
Jesus, Mary and Joseph, assist me in my last agony.
Jesus, Mary and Joseph, may I breathe forth my soul in peace with you.
Amen.

OTHER PRAYERS

ALL-POWERFUL and merciful Father, in the death of Christ you have opened a gateway to eternal life. Look kindly upon our brother/sister who is suffering his/her last agony. United to the passion and death of your Son, and saved by the blood he shed, may he/she come before you with confidence. Through the same Christ our Lord. Amen.

MARY, Mother of God, who stood by the cross as our Lord and Saviour died, be the comfort and advocate of N. who is so shortly to come before the same Lord, your dear Son, and of all those who love him/her. Hold them all in your tender arms, and pray for them that are to be separated for a while; may they all meet again in God's kingdom united in joy and love with the Blessed Trinity, who live and reign for ever and ever. Amen.

The Rosary is often a valuable prayer to use at a deathbed; its rhythms are comforting, and its repetitive nature helps those who find it difficult to concentrate on account of the circumstances.

AT THE MOMENT OF DEATH

Roman Ritual, tr. John Henry Newman

GO forth upon thy journey, Christian soul!
Go from this world! Go, in the name of God
The omnipotent Father, who created thee!
Go, in the name of Jesus Christ, our Lord,
Son of the living God, who bled for thee!
Go, in the Name of the Holy Spirit, who
Hath been poured out on thee! Go, in the name
Of Angels and Archangels; in the name
Of Thrones and Dominations; in the name
Of Princedoms and of Powers; and in the name
Of Cherubim and Seraphim, go forth!
Go, in the name of Patriarchs and Prophets,
And of Apostles and Evangelists,
Of Martyrs and Confessors; in the name
Of holy Monks and Hermits; in the name
Of holy Virgins, and all Saints of God,
Both men and women, go! Go on thy course;
And may thy place to-day be found in peace,
And may thy dwelling be the Holy Mount
Of Sion—through the Same, through Christ, our Lord.

MERCIFUL God, forgiving God, O God who forget the transgressions of the repentant sinner, look kindly on this your servant N. who returns to you, his/her Creator, and who begs forgiveness of his/her sins. Do not deny his/her humble prayer! Re-create him/her anew; rebuild that which was marred, repair that which was broken, make beautiful that which was defiled, fortify that which was made frail.

We, the Church militant on earth entrust this our brother/sister to the care of the Church Triumphant in heaven where, assisted by the prayers and suffrages of his/her brethren, we pray that he/she may be quickly joined with the saints and angels to praise you for ever and ever. Amen.

Nunc Dimittis

Luke 2:29–32

LORD, now let your servant depart in peace,
      according to your promise;
   for my eyes have seen your salvation
   which you have prepared in the sight of all peoples,
a light for revelation to the Gentiles,
      and for glory to your people Israel.

Eternal rest grant unto him/her, O Lord,
      and let perpetual light shine upon him/her.

Psalm 129: De Profundis

The traditional, 'Douai' translation.

OUT OF the depths I have cried unto thee O Lord:
      Lord, hear my voice.
   Let thine ears be attentive:
   to the voice of my supplication.
If thou, O Lord, shalt observe iniquities
   Lord, who shall endure it?
For with thee there is merciful forgiveness:
   and by reason of thy law I have waited for thee, O Lord.
My soul hath waited on his word:
   my soul hath hoped in the Lord.
From the morning watch even unto night
   let Israel hope in the Lord.

For with the Lord there is mercy:
    and with him is plentiful redemption.
And he shall redeem Israel:
    from all his iniquities.

℣. Eternal rest grant unto them, O Lord.
℞. **And let perpetual light shine upon them.**

℣. May they rest in peace.
℞. **Amen.**

℣. O Lord, hear my prayer.
℞. **And let my cry come unto thee.**

Let us pray.

O GOD, the Creator and Redeemer of all the faithful; grant to the souls of thy servants departed the remission of all their sins, that through pious supplications they may obtain the pardon which they have always desired. Who livest and reignest world without end. Amen.

ANOTHER TRANSLATION

OUT OF the depths I cry to you O Lord:
    Lord, hear my voice.
    O may your ears be attentive:
    to the voice of my pleading.
O Lord, if you will keep count of our sins
    Lord, who could bear it?
For with you there is merciful forgiveness:
    that yet we might serve you.
My soul is waiting for you, O Lord:
    my soul is longing for a word from him.
My soul is hoping in the Lord
    more than the watchman for the dawn.
More than the watchman for the dawn
    let Israel hope in the Lord.
For with the Lord there is mercy,
    and with him is abundant redemption.
And he shall redeem Israel from every one of its sins.

℣. Eternal rest grant unto them, O Lord.

℟. And let perpetual light shine upon them.

℣. May they rest in peace.

℟. Amen.

℣. O Lord, hear my prayer.

℟. And let my cry come to you.

Let us pray.

O GOD, the Creator and Redeemer of all the faithful: grant to the souls of your servants departed forgiveness of all their sins, that through our earnest prayers they may obtain the pardon which they have always desired. Who live and reign for ever and ever. Amen.

A Byzantine Prayer

G OD of all spirits and of all flesh, who trampled upon death, and overthrew the devil, giving life to the world: O Lord, grant rest to the soul of your departed servant N., in a place of light, in a place of pasture, in a place of rest, from whence pain, sadness and tears have all fled; and forgive him/her all sins, whether committed in thought, word or deed, O good God, lover of humanity; for there is no one living who is sinless: you alone are without sin; your justice is eternal justice, and your word is truth. For you yourself are the resurrection, and the life, and the rest of your departed servant N., O Christ our God; and to you we offer glory, together with your eternal Father, and your most holy, good, and life-giving Spirit, now, and always, and for ages unending. Amen.

O DIVINE Lord, whose adorable heart ardently sighs for the happiness of your children, we humbly pray that you remember the souls of your servants for whom we pray; command that your holy angels receive them and convey them to a place of rest and peace. Amen.

MAY the bright company of angels bear your soul to Paradise. May the glorious band of apostles greet you at the gates. May the white-robed army of martyrs welcome you. May the cheerful throngs of saints lighten your heart for ever. May those you have loved and lost be glad of your coming. May Mary enfold you in her tender arms, and lead you to Jesus your love for ever, and for whom you have longed all this while. May your home be in the heavenly Jerusalem this day and for ever. Rest in peace, N. God keep you in his care. Amen.

O GOD, whose nature is always to have mercy and to spare, we humbly pray to you for the soul of your servant N. whom you have this day called out of the world, that you would not deliver him/her up into the hands of the enemy, nor forget him/her eternally, but command him/her to be received by your holy angels, and to be carried to Paradise, his/her true country; that as in you N. had faith and hope he/she may not suffer the pains of loss, but may take possession of everlasting joys. Through Christ our Lord. Amen.

MAY the souls of the faithful departed, through the mercy of God, rest in peace. Amen.

THE BEREAVED

A Blessing

to be used after any of the following prayers and readings.

MAY Christ, who comforts us in all our tribulations, support you in your trial and bring you peace. May he, who wept at the grave of Lazarus, be your comforter and wipe away all tears from your eyes. May almighty God bless you and keep you in his care: Father, Son ✠ and Holy Spirit. Amen.

Elderly Bereaved

A reading from the Book of Job.   19:23–27

WHO will grant me that my words may be written? Who will grant me that they may be marked down in a book with an iron pen, or else be graven with an instrument in flint? For I know that my Redeemer lives, and in the last day I shall rise out of the earth, and I shall be clothed again with my skin and in my flesh I shall see my God. I myself shall see him, and my eyes shall behold him and not another: this my hope is laid up in my heart.

Let us pray.

BE with us, Lord, in this time of sadness and parting. We pray your mercy for the soul of N. and your comfort for those who mourn him/her; though this parting be full of sadness, may this sorrow turn to joy on that day when we, together with N., all shall arise and, our youth, health, and beauty being restored, in our flesh look upon you, the living God. Through Christ our risen Lord. Amen.

Sudden Death

A reading from the book of Wisdom. 4:7–15

THE just man, though he be cut off in death, shall be at rest, for venerability is not from living a long life, nor counted by the number of years; a man's understanding is his grey hairs, a spotless life is old age. He pleased God and was beloved, and so since he lived among sinners he was removed; taken away lest wickedness should alter his understanding or deceit beguile his soul. For vanity bewitches and obscures good things, and the wandering of concupiscence overturns the innocent mind. So being made perfect in a short space, he lived a long life, for his soul pleased God; therefore he hastened to bring him out of the midst of iniquities. The people see this, but do not understand; their hearts cannot grasp that the grace of God and his mercy is with his saints and that he looks upon his chosen.

Let us pray.

DEAR Lord, help us to understand what has just happened. We understand that you are a good and loving God, that you see a sparrow's fall, and that even the hairs on our head are counted; help us to make sense of what seems to us to be a senseless tragedy. Restore and strengthen our faith in your Divine Providence, and grant rest and pardon to N. whom we love, and whom we entrust to your loving arms. Through Christ our Lord. Amen.

Suicide

A reading from the letter of St Paul to the Romans. 8:35–39

WHAT then shall separate us from the love of Christ? Shall tribulation, or distress, or famine, or nakedness, or danger, or persecution, or the sword? ... But in all these things we overcome because of him who has loved us. For I am sure that neither death, nor life, nor angels, nor principalities, nor powers, nor things present, nor things to come, nor might, nor height, nor depth, nor any other creature shall be able to separate us from the love of God, which is in Christ Jesus our Lord.

Let us pray.

DEAREST Father, we commend to your loving mercy your child, and our brother/sister N. who has died in such a tragic way. We cannot understand or judge what may have been his/her state of mind, and so we pray with all our hearts that N. may speedily find a place of forgiveness, rest and peace in your Sacred Heart that was pierced with the lance for his/her salvation. And, heavenly Father, grant comfort and understanding to those who loved N. and grieve at his/her death. We ask this through Christ our Lord. Amen.

For a Non-Believer

A reading from the letter of St Paul to the Romans. 14:7–9

NONE of us lives to himself, and no one dies to himself. For whether we live, we live to the Lord, or whether we die, we die to the Lord. Therefore, whether we live, or whether we die, we are the Lord's. For to this end Christ died and rose again; that he might be Lord both of the dead and of the living.

Let us pray.

HEAVENLY Father, we understand that you are the Father of all humanity, and that nothing is beyond your love or your mercy. We pray that you receive in your tender arms N. who has not known you in this life, but now knows you better than we who remain. Let him/her know all the goodness of the God who has watched over him/her in this life, forgive his/her failings and admit him/her to the company of the blessed. We ask this through Christ our Lord. Amen.

Miscarriage / Still birth

A reading from the prophet Jeremiah. 1:4

BEFORE I formed you in the womb of your mother, I knew you: and before you came forth from the womb, I consecrated you.

and/or

A reading from the holy Gospel according to Matthew. 10:29–31

ARE not two sparrows sold for a farthing? Not one of them shall fall to the ground without your Father knowing; the very hairs of your head are all numbered. Do not be afraid, therefore: you are worth more than many sparrows.

A T this sad time, Lord, we bring our sorrow before you and ask for your healing, and your enlightenment. Our little child has already had a place in our love and our hearts; now we entrust our baby [whom we name N.] into your loving arms, knowing that you will be an even more loving and caring parent than ever we could be in this life. And for us who remain here on earth, assuage our grief and strengthen our faith in your goodness and your care for all whom you have made. Through Christ our Lord. Amen.

May almighty God bless us all, the Father, the Son ✠ and the Holy Spirit. Amen.

and/or

Let us pray.

L ORD God, strengthen our faith that nothing in your creation is without value in your sight, that all you make has meaning and is loved by you. Be a father to our little one, we pray you; grant him/ her in abundance that love which we were unable to show on earth. Help us to see your loving hand in what has happened; strengthen our faith and, if it be your will, grant that we may one day see and love this child of yours who has returned to you before even drawing breath. Lord God, source of all life and love, be with us at this time for our comfort and our solace. Through Christ our Lord. Amen.

TRAVEL AND MIGRATION

꧁ ⚓ ꧂

THE ITINERARIUM
ANCIENT PRAYER BEFORE A JOURNEY

Antiphon: In the way of peace and prosperity may the Lord, the Almighty and merciful, direct our steps. And may the angel Raphael accompany us on our way, that we may return to our home in peace, safety and joy.

B LESSED ✠ be the Lord, the God of Israel,
 who has visited and redeemed his people,
And has lifted up a horn of salvation for us
 in the family of his servant David.
For this he swore through the mouths of holy men:
 those who were prophets, from the beginning:
There would be salvation from our foes,
 and from the hand of all those who hate us;
to comfort our fathers,
 and to honour his holy covenant,
which oath once he swore to Abraham, our father,
 that he would grant us,
that freed from the hand of our enemies,
 and without fear, we may serve him,
 in holiness and justice in his very presence all our days.
And you, my son, will be named Prophet of the Most High;
 for you will go before the presence of the Lord
 to prepare his way,
to teach knowledge of salvation to his people
 that their sins may be forgiven,
 through the merciful heart of our God,
when the Daystar shall visit us from on high
 to enlighten those who sit in darkness
 and in the shadow of death,
 and guide our feet to the way of peace.
Glory be …

Antiphon: In the way of peace and prosperity may the Lord, the Almighty and merciful, direct our steps. And may the angel Raphael accompany us on our way, that we may return to our home in peace, safety and joy.

Lord, have mercy.
Christ, have mercy.
Lord, have mercy.

Our Father.

℣. O Lord, save your servants,
℟. Who trust in you, O God.

℣. Send us help, O Lord, from your holy place,
℟. And defend us out of Sion.

℣. Be unto us, O Lord, a tower of strength,
℟. From the face of the enemy.

℣. Do not let the enemy prevail against us.
℟. Nor let evil-doers approach to hurt us.

℣. Blessed be the Lord from day to day.
℟. God our salvation, make our way prosper before us.

℣. Show us your ways, O Lord,
℟. And teach us your paths.

℣. O, that our footsteps may be directed
℟. To keeping your righteous laws.

℣. The crooked ways shall be made straight,
℟. And the rough places smooth.

℣. God has given his angels charge over you,
℟. To keep you on your way.

℣. O Lord, hear my prayer,
℟. And let my cry come before you.

Let us pray.

O GOD, who made the sons of Israel to walk with dry feet through the midst of the sea, and who opened to the three magi, by the guiding of a star, the way which led to your Son: grant to us, we beg, a prosperous journey and a time of tranquillity, that, attended by your holy angels, we may happily arrive at N., and finally at the haven of eternal salvation.

O GOD, who brought Abraham your son out of the land of the Chaldees, and preserved him unhurt through all his journeyings, we beseech you to keep us your servants safe; be to us our support in our setting out, our solace on the way, our shade in the heat, our shelter in the rain and cold, our transport in our weariness, our fortress in trouble, our staff on slippery paths, our harbour on stormy seas, that under your guidance we may safely reach our destination, and at length return home in safety.

L ISTEN, O Lord, we beg, to our prayers, and arrange the way of your servants in the blessedness of your salvation, that amidst all the various changes of this our life and pilgrimage, we may ever be protected by your help.

G RANT to your people, we beg you, almighty God, that they may walk onward in the way of salvation, and by following the exhortations of blessed John the Baptist, the forerunner, that they may come safely to the presence of the One of whom John spoke, Jesus Christ your Son, our Lord, who lives and reigns with you in the unity of the Holy Spirit, one God for ever and ever. Amen.

℣. Let us proceed on our journey in peace.
℟. **In the name of the Lord. Amen.**

For Those About to Emigrate

O GOD, who sent your servant Joseph into Egypt to find food for his family in a time of famine, and did fulfil their need through his sacrifice, be the merciful guard and guide to this servant of yours (these servants of yours) who are leaving this land to seek a new home and a fuller life elsewhere. Prosper all he/she does (they do), keep him/her/them in your care, and give him/her/them all they need to settle in their new home; may we all meet again one day in that heaven which is our common homeland, and see you face to face, where you live and reign for ever and ever. Amen.

For New Immigrants

O GOD, who lived in a land of exile, and who commanded that we welcome the stranger, grant your grace to us all to welcome new friends and family, that they may soon find their feet among us and bring their own particular gifts to enrich our lives as we share what we have with them.

N., be welcome among us not as a stranger, but as beloved new family.

DISTRESS OF MIND

FOR FORGIVENESS

A reading from the Gospel according to Luke.   15:12–24

JESUS said: 'A certain man had two sons. And the younger of them said to his father: "Father, give me the share of the inheritance that will come to me [when you die]." And he divided his substance between them. And not many days after, the younger son, gathering everything together, went abroad into a far country, and there wasted his substance, living riotously. And after he had spent everything, there came a mighty famine in that country: and he began to be in need. So he went and joined one of the citizens of that country, who sent him into his farm to feed pigs. And he would happily have filled his belly with the husks the swine were eating, but no one gave him anything. And coming to himself, he said: "How many hired servants in my father's house have more than enough bread, and here I perish with hunger! I will arise and will go to my father and say to him: 'Father, I have sinned against heaven and before you. I am not worthy to be called your son: make me as one of your hired servants.'" And rising up, he went home to his father. And when he was still a long way off, his father saw him and was moved with compassion and running to him fell upon his neck and kissed him. And the son said to him: "Father, I have sinned against heaven and before you; I am not now worthy to be called your son." And the father said to his servants: "Bring quickly the best robe and put it on him: and put a ring on his hand and shoes on his feet. And bring here the fatted calf, and kill it: and let us eat and make merry: Because this my son was dead and is come to life again, was lost and is found." And they began to be merry.'

Let us pray.

HEAVENLY Father, whom we have hurt by our sins, we know that we are not worthy to be called your children; we cannot pretend before you that we are anything other than what we are, because you can read our hearts and know even better than we do just what lies within us. But from the words of Jesus we know that if we are truly repentant, even if some of the damage we have done cannot be repaired, we can be again your beloved children. Help us to return home with all our hearts, home, where we truly belong, and be determined never to leave your love again. Through Christ our Lord. Amen.

A reading from the letter of St Paul to the Romans.   8:32–39

IF God be for us, who can be against us? He that did not spare even his own Son, but delivered him up for us all, how has he not also, with him, given us all things? Who shall accuse the elect of God? God is the one who justifies: Who is he that shall condemn? [Only] Christ Jesus who died and who has risen again, who is at the right hand of God, who also makes intercession for us. And what then shall separate us from the love of Christ? Shall tribulation? Or distress? Or famine? Or nakedness? Or danger? Or persecution? Or the sword? (As it is written: For your sake, we are put to death all the day long. We are accounted as sheep for the slaughter.) But in all these things we overcome, because of him who has loved us. For I am sure that neither death, nor life, nor angels, nor principalities, nor powers, nor things present, nor things to come, nor might, nor height, nor depth, nor any other creature, shall be able to separate us from the love of God which is in Christ Jesus our Lord.

Let us pray.

HEAVENLY Father, we know we are precious in your sight, that you have even counted every hair on our head. We know we have offended you countless times, and yet your mercy is such that even the worst sinner can become your most beloved child. Help us to feel something of that same love; help us to feel that you are near; to comfort us when we are sorrowful, to be our company when we are lonely, our refuge in grief, and in the end to see ourselves as you see us: worth dying for. Through Christ our Lord. Amen.

ADDICTION

A reading from the letter of St Paul to the Romans.   8:32–39

IF God be for us, who can be against us? He who did not spare even his own Son, but delivered him up for us all, how has he not also, with him, given us all things? Who shall accuse the elect of God? God is the one who justifies: Who is he that shall condemn? [Only] Christ Jesus who died and who has risen again, who is at the right hand of God, who also makes intercession for us. And what then shall separate us from the love of Christ? Shall tribulation? Or distress? Or famine? Or nakedness? Or danger? Or persecution? Or the sword? (As it is written: For your sake, we are put to death all the day long. We are accounted as sheep for the slaughter.) But in all these things we overcome, because of him who has loved us. For I am sure that neither death, nor life, nor angels, nor principalities, nor powers, nor things present, nor things to come, nor might, nor height, nor depth, nor any other creature, shall be able to separate us from the love of God which is in Christ Jesus our Lord.

L ORD God, master of the Universe and Creator of all that is, we pray your strength and blessing for N. who is struggling with addiction to [...]. Lord Jesus Christ, the Key of David, loose the chains that bind N., open the gates of his/her prison that he/she may serve you in perfect freedom. Holy Spirit, breathe into N. your own fresh air that blows where it will; grant him/her the necessary self-confidence, self-control and self-mastery to defeat this problem which afflicts him/her, who live and reign for ever and ever. Amen.

With the Family of an Addict

O GOD, our loving Father, you understand and forgive the frailty of your children. We ask you now to extend your strong arm in blessing over N. Help him/her to believe that faith overcomes the weakness of human nature, and that your grace will sustain him/her in the struggle to be free of the power and influence of [...]. Help him/her to seek and find in you a rock and a refuge in times of difficulty and temptation, and make him/her aware of your ever-loving presence in his/her life. Through Christ our Lord. Amen,

PAROCHIAL AND DIOCESAN NEEDS

For More Help from Laity

O LORD, who sent seventy disciples before you into those towns and villages that you were to visit, we ask your blessing on the pastoral endeavours of this parish/diocese, and grant us those faithful fellow-workers we need so that the Kingdom of God may be extended in this place, and your name better known and served. Through Christ our Lord. Amen.

L ORD Jesus, grant us that help which we cannot provide for ourselves. Since by our baptism, and in our reception of Holy Communion, you have made us your mystical body on earth, grant us the active and helpful members we need to do what you would do, go where you would go, and say what you would say. Send us not just those who are willing, but also those who are capable to do the jobs that need to be done, efficiently and without fuss; peaceable and not contentious folk who will enable this parish/diocese to further your kingdom on earth, who live and reign for ever and ever. Amen.

Building or Restoring a Church

A LMIGHTY God, who did command your servants David and Solomon to build a temple for you, and who have built your faithful followers into a living temple, fit for your solemn praise; mercifully hear our prayers for this building enterprise we have undertaken, and see it to its completion, that you may be more fittingly worshipped in this place. Through Christ our Lord. Amen.

H EAVENLY Father, we ask your blessing on the beginning (continuation) of our project. Since we have launched out in faith, we ask that this faith be not misplaced, and that our hope not deceive us. We trust you to find us the money we need, and to guide the hands of artisan and craftsman, that all may be done to your greater glory, and our salvation. May the completed work be a prayer in stone/ brick that all may see the love we bear for you, who live and reign for ever and ever. Amen.

DISSENSION

A reading from the letter of St Paul to the Philippians. 4:4–9

REJOICE in the Lord always: again, I say, rejoice. Let your forebearance be known to all men. The Lord is near. Do not be worried, but in everything, by prayer and supplication with thanksgiving, let your petitions be made known to God. And may the peace of God, which surpasses all understanding, keep your hearts and minds in Christ Jesus. For the rest, brethren, whatever things are true, whatever modest, whatever just, whatever holy, whatever lovely, whatever of good repute; if there be any virtue, if anything praiseworthy: think on these things. The things which you have both learned and received and heard and seen in me, do them, and the God of peace shall be with you.

Let us pray.

ALMIGHTY God, all of whose ways are peace and concord, and who maintain all creation in order and stasis, we pray for that peace which the world cannot give, that our hearts may be undividedly given to you, who are the source of eternal life. Through Christ our Lord. Amen.

HEAL our sad divisions, Lord Jesus Christ, who came to reconcile sinners and call them to your Sacred Heart. May there be peace and reconciliation between us who all desire to serve you and further your Kingdom. Help us to find a way through this difficulty which will be pleasing to all and especially to you, who live and reign for ever and ever. Amen.

MEETINGS

Parish Councils

A reading from the holy Gospel according to Matthew.   18:19–20

JESUS said to his disciples: I say to you, that if two of you shall consent upon earth, concerning any thing whatsoever they shall ask, it shall be done to them by my Father who is in heaven. For where there are two or three gathered together in my name, there am I in the midst of them.

Let us pray.

HOLY Spirit, fill our hearts with your charity and our minds with your wisdom as we meet today/tonight. Fill us with sufficient grace to be honest and fair in our deliberations, but keep us from all useless argument. Let us speak solely from motives of love, having at all times the interest of our parish at heart. May we seek only the glory of God and the growth of his kingdom here in [place]. May our Lady [and St *Patron*] pray for us and for all the members of this parish, that we may grow closer to God and to one another, becoming each day more worthy disciples of our Lord Jesus Christ, who lives and reigns with you and the Father, one God for ever and ever. Amen.

A Meeting Likely to be Stormy

A reading from the letter of St Paul to the Romans.   14:7–13, 17–19

NONE of us lives to himself, and no one dies to himself, for whether we live or whether we die, we are the Lord's. For to this end Christ died and rose again; that he might be Lord both of the dead and of the living. So why do you judge your brother? Or you, why do you despise your brother? We shall, after all, all stand before the judgment seat of Christ. For as it is written: As I live, says the Lord, every knee shall bow to me, and every tongue shall acknowledge God. Therefore every one of us shall render account to God for himself. Let us not therefore judge one another any more, but rather be careful that you do not put a stumbling block or a scandal in your brother's way ... For the kingdom of God is not food and drink, but justice, and peace, and joy in the

Holy Spirit. For he that serves Christ in this pleases God, and is approved of by men. So let us follow after the things that are of peace, and keep to the things that give edification to one another.

Let us pray.

SEND forth your own peace upon us, O Lord, and grant us wisdom and charity in abundance, that our business this day may be transacted calmly to the profit of all, and to the furtherance of your Kingdom, where you live and reign for ever and ever. Amen.

A Meeting for Some Sad Duty

A reading from the second letter of St Paul to the Corinthians.   1:3–7

BLESSED be the God and Father of our Lord Jesus Christ, the Father of mercies and the God of all comfort, who comforts us in all our tribulations, that we also may be able to comfort those who are in all distress, by the encouragement with which we also are encouraged by God. For as the sufferings of Christ abound in us: so also by Christ our comfort abounds too. So when we are in tribulation, it is for your encouragement and salvation: and when we are comforted, it is for your consolation: and when we are encouraged, it is for your encouragement and salvation, which brings about endurance of the same sufferings which we also suffer. So that our hope for you may be sure, we know that as you are sharers of our suffering, so shall you share also in the consolation.

Let us pray.

STRENGTHEN us, O Lord, with your mighty power, and send from on high your Holy Spirit, the Consoler, to inspire what we do and say this day. Fortify us in your service that we may do what needs to be done without prevarication, and without violating your sacred law of charity towards you and our neighbour. Through Christ our Lord. Amen.

A Meeting for Some Happy Duty

A reading from the letter of St Paul to the Philippians. 4:4–9

REJOICE in the Lord always: again, I say, rejoice. Let your forebearance be known to all men. The Lord is near. Do not be worried, but in everything, by prayer and supplication, with thanksgiving, let your petitions be made known to God. And may the peace of God, which surpasses all understanding, keep your hearts and minds in Christ Jesus. For the rest, brethren, whatever things are true, whatever modest, whatever just, whatever holy, whatever lovely, whatever of good repute; if there be any virtue, if anything praiseworthy: think on these things. The things which you have both learned and received and heard and seen in me, do them, and the God of peace shall be with you.

Let us pray.

GREAT God of goodness, whose love for us exceeds anything we could deserve, we ask your blessing on this meeting, and your inspiration for all we will say and enact. In all things, may we reflect your own generosity, who did not even deny us your only Son, who lives and reigns with you and the Holy Spirit, God for ever and ever. Amen.

Meetings in General

A reading from the letter of St James. 3:17–18

THE wisdom that is from above is first chaste, then peaceable, modest, easily persuaded of the truth, consenting to the good, full of mercy and good fruits, without condemnation, without dissimulation; and the fruit of justice is sown in peace to those who make peace.

Before meetings

COME, Holy Spirit, fill the hearts of your faithful, and kindle in them the fire of your love.

℣. Send forth your Spirit and they shall be created.
℟. **And you will renew the face of the earth.**

Lord, have mercy,	**Lord, have mercy.**
Christ, have mercy,	**Christ, have mercy.**
Lord, have mercy.	**Lord, have mercy.**

Our Father.

℣. Remember your people, O Lord,
℟. **Who have been yours from of old.**
℣. O Lord, hear my prayer,
℟. **And let my cry come to you.**

Let us pray.

ILLUMINE our minds, we beseech you, Lord, with the light of your glory, that we may be enabled to see what needs to be done, and be empowered to see it soon and fruitfully effected. Through Christ our Lord. Amen.

After meetings

Lord, have mercy,	**Lord, have mercy.**
Christ, have mercy,	**Christ, have mercy.**
Lord, have mercy.	**Lord, have mercy.**

Our Father.

℣. Strengthen, O God, what has been done among us.
℟. **And give us help from your holy temple.**
℣. O Lord, hear my prayer,
℟. **And let my cry come to you.**

Let us pray.

GRANT us, O Lord, the help of your grace, that since we have deliberated by the help of your inspiration, we may continue to acknowledge you, the author of all good, and thus see our good resolutions put into effect. Through Christ our Lord. Amen.

Adsumus: Before Meetings

W E have come, O Lord, Holy Spirit, we have come before you hampered indeed by our many and grievous sins, but for a special purpose gathered together in your name. Come to us and be with us and enter our hearts.

Teach us what we are to do and where we ought to tend; show us what we must accomplish, in order that, with your help, we may be able to please you in all things.

May you alone be the author and the finisher of our judgements, who alone with God the Father and his Son possess a glorious name.

Do not allow us to disturb the order of justice, since you love equity above all things. Let not ignorance draw us into devious paths. Let not partiality sway our minds or respect of riches or persons pervert our judgement.

But unite us to you effectually by the gift of your grace alone, that we may be one in you and never forsake the truth; inasmuch as we are gathered together in your name, so may we in all things hold fast to justice tempered by mercy, so that in this life our judgement may in no wise be at variance with you and in the life to come we may attain to everlasting rewards for deeds well done. Amen.

Another Prayer Before Meetings
WHEN A LIGHTER TOUCH IS REQUIRED

H EAVENLY Father, be present with us now. Let all our deliberations tend to your glory and the furtherance of the Gospel. Let our discussions be charitable and our conclusions fruitful. May the breeze of your Holy Spirit breathe among us instead of long-windedness, let there be no fighting of corners or sacrificing long-term trust for short-term popularity. In short, dear Father, may this meeting end on time, with your kingdom furthered. Through the one who used few words but to great effect, Jesus Christ our Lord. Amen.

EDUCATION

❦ ✠ ❦

Sunday Schools or Catechism Classes

Holy Spirit, make us wise,
Holy Spirit, make us holy,
Holy Spirit, help us understand,
Holy Spirit, help us attend.

Holy Mary, teach us goodness,
Holy Mary, teach us to love your Son,
Holy Mary, teach us the way to heaven. Amen.

The Catechist of the Young
for him or herself

Enchiridion

JESUS, lover of the young, who were seen from tender years to grow in wisdom and grace before God and mankind; who at twelve years old sat among the doctors in the temple, attentively listening and humbly questioning, they being surprised at the prudence and wisdom of your words; who delighted to receive children and bless them, saying to your disciples 'Let them come to me; of such is the kingdom of heaven': Inspire me, like St Peter Canisius, to be a perfect example of a catechist, and a good leader. May I have a profound reverence and a holy love for the children, a willing inclination to teach them the study of Christian doctrine, and a special skill in these things that they may understand its mysteries, and love its beauty. Lord Jesus, this I pray, and ask the intercession of the Blessed Virgin Mary. Amen.

Primary / Grade Schools

A New Term

HEAVENLY Father, as we begin a new term help us to really do our best.
Help us to be kind and generous to our friends, and patient and friendly with those we dislike;
May we listen carefully to our teachers,
  and do as they ask without arguing,
  and not talk when they are talking,
  and not shout out, but put up our hands if we want something.
because this is about being kind and respectful to other people,
and we know that you want us to be kind and respectful.
May we say our prayers well, and really mean them.
May we love you, and our Lady and our Patron Saints (especially St N.) with all our hearts.
We ask all this through Christ our Lord. Amen.

Secondary / High Schools

A reading from the book of Proverbs.   4:1–13

HEAR, children, the instruction of a father, and listen that you may know prudence. I will give you a good gift, do not forsake my law. For I also was my father's son, young and like an only son in the sight of my mother: And he taught me, and said: Let your heart receive my words, keep my commandments, and you shall live. Learn wisdom, learn prudence: do not forget, nor depart from the words of my mouth. Do not forsake wisdom, and she will keep you: love her, and she will preserve you. The beginning of wisdom is the acquisition of wisdom, and with all you possess, purchase prudence. Take hold of her, and she will exalt you: you will be glorified by her when you embrace her. She will give to your head increase of graces, and protect you with a noble crown. Hear, my son, and receive my words, that the years of your life may be multiplied. I will show you the way of wisdom, I will lead you by the paths of equity: When you have entered them, your steps shall not be constrained, and when you run, you will not meet a stumbling block. Take hold on instruction, do not leave it: keep it, because it is your life.

ONCE more, dear Lord, we take up our academic endeavours. We ask your blessing on this new term; may we work diligently, understand thoroughly, and grow in stature and grace in your sight, and that of our neighbours.

Holy Spirit, fill us with your wisdom and power. Teach us the right use of knowledge and growing strength; help us to keep things in proportion and to see that gaining heaven is the final purpose of all we do here, and so that everything we shall do this term is relative to that great goal.

But in the meantime, may we study diligently, play enthusiastically, courteously interact with others and find even now that life is worth living when it is lived well and to the full. Through Christ our Lord. Amen.

℣. Our Lady, seat of wisdom,
℟. **Pray for us.**
℣. St Thomas More,
℟. **Pray for us.**

BEFORE EXAMINATIONS

Perhaps the most appropriate setting for a pre-exam prayer would be a votive Mass of the Holy Spirit. Otherwise, a simple prayer such as the following could be said before the students begin.

COME, Holy Spirit and enlighten all those about to undergo these examinations; refresh their memories and sharpen their minds that all who are tested may truly do themselves justice, and thus not only better themselves, but further the kingdom of our Lord Jesus Christ, to whom be honour and glory for ever and ever. Amen.

LORD God, help us to read the questions well;
to understand what we have read;
to stay calm and untroubled;

to pace ourselves;
to remember accurately;
to think clearly;
and to express our thoughts lucidly;
for your name's sake. Amen.

℣. Our Lady, seat of wisdom,
℟. **Pray for us.**
℣. St Thomas Aquinas,
℟. **Pray for us.**

Universities and Colleges

At graduation

A reading from the book of Wisdom.   7:7–26

I PRAYED, and wisdom was given me: I called upon God, and the spirit of wisdom came upon me. And I preferred her before kingdoms and thrones, and esteemed riches as nothing in comparison with her. Neither can I compare with her any precious stone, for in comparison gold is as a little sand, and silver in respect to her can be counted as clay. I loved her above health and beauty, and chose to have her instead of light, for her light cannot be put out. Now all good things came to me together with her, and innumerable riches through her hands, and I rejoiced in all these, for this wisdom went before me, and I did not know that she was the mother of them all. What I have learned without guile, may I communicate without envy, and not hide her riches. For she is an infinite treasure to humanity; those who use her become the friends of God, commended for the gifts of teaching.

Now may God grant me to speak as he wishes, and to think thoughts worthy of what I have learnt, for he is the guide of wisdom and the director of the wise. Both we and our words are in his hands, and so is all wisdom, and the knowledge of how things work; he has given me true knowledge of the things that are; the disposition of the whole world, and the virtues of the elements; the beginning and ending and midst of times, the alterations of their courses, and the changing of the seasons, the revolutions of the years and the positions of the stars, the natures of living creatures, and the rage of wild beasts, the force of winds and the reasonings of men, the diversities of plants, and the virtues of roots: all such things which are yet undiscovered I have learned, for wisdom, which works all things, taught me.

For in her is the spirit of understanding: holy, one, manifold, subtle, eloquent, active, undefiled, sure, sweet, loving that which is good, alive, irresistible, beneficent, gentle, kind, steadfast, assured, secure, all-powerful, overseeing all things, intelligent, pure, deep. She is the spirit of the power of God, and a certain pure emanation of the glory of the almighty God, and therefore nothing defiled comes into her. For she is the brightness of eternal light, and the unspotted mirror of God's majesty, and the image of his goodness.

Let us pray.

ALMIGHTY God, we give you most grateful thanks for what we have learnt, and what we have achieved. As this phase of our lives draws to its end, we pray that our knowledge may pass into wisdom which will contribute to the betterment of this world, to the end that we may be saved in the world to come.

We give thanks, too, for the friends we have made here, and for the range of many good experiences that have come our way during these last few years.

Finally, we pray that the qualifications we have achieved may be of real help to us in the future, to secure happy and fulfilling employment. May we always look back on our time here at this University with pleasure, and remember it in our generosity and in our prayers. Through Christ our Lord. Amen.

EDUCATIONAL FOUNDATION STONE LAYING

A reading from the letter of St Paul to the Ephesians.   3:14–21

I BOW my knees to the Father of our Lord Jesus Christ, after whom all families in heaven and earth are named, that he would grant you, according to the riches of his glory, to be strengthened by his Spirit with might in the inner man; that Christ may dwell by faith in your hearts: so that, being rooted and founded in charity, you may be able to comprehend, with all the saints, what is the breadth and length and height and depth, and to know also the love of Christ, which surpasses all knowledge: that you may be filled with all the fulness of God. Now to him who according to the power that works in us is able to do all things more abundantly than we could desire or understand, to him be glory in the church and in Christ Jesus, unto all generations, world without end. Amen.

Let us pray.

L ORD Jesus Christ, the wisdom of God and precious Corner Stone, bless ✠, we pray, this foundation stone, also the building which will arise upon it, and all those who will work and study here. May this place be built swiftly and safely, and come to completion in due time, to your glory and our benefit. And may all that we do or say have you as its inspiration, its guide and its end, that we may all come one day to the Kingdom where you reign with your Father and the Holy Spirit, God for ever and ever. Amen.

A New Classroom

H EAVENLY Father, our first and greatest teacher, we thank you for the completion of this new part of our school. We ask that you bless all the work which will take place here, and grant us, staff and pupils, to learn all those things that you wish us to; not just how to count and spell, but how to love you, and our neighbour as ourselves. May we learn the greatness of your teachings above all, and as we learn about this beautiful world that you have made, make us fit disciples of your kingdom where you live and reign for ever and ever. Amen.

May this classroom be blessed in the name of the Father, and of the Son, ✠ and of the Holy Spirit. Amen.

Before an Adult Education Class

A reading from the book of Wisdom. 39:6–10

T HE wise man will give his heart to rise early to seek the Lord that made him, and he will pray in the sight of the Most High. He will open his mouth in prayer, and will make supplication for his sins. And if it shall please the great Lord, he will fill him with the spirit of understanding, and he will pour forth the words of his wisdom like showers, and in his prayer he will give thanks to the Lord. And the Lord shall rightly direct his counsel, and his knowledge, and on the Lord's secrets shall he meditate. He will show others the wisdom he has learnt, and shall glory in the law of the covenant of the Lord. Many shall praise his wisdom, and it shall never be forgotten; the memory of him shall not fade, and his name shall be remembered from generation to generation.

Let us pray.

HOLY Spirit, inspire all we say and do this day; sharpen our wits to study with profit, to speak and listen clearly, to communicate and to understand, that what we learn we may also share with others, to the furtherance of your kingdom, where you live and reign for ever and ever. Amen.

Before a Confirmation Class

O GOD, who have taught the hearts of the faithful by the light of the Holy Spirit, grant that we may be truly wise and ever rejoice in his consolations. Through Christ our Lord. Amen.

MAY the God of all grace who has called you to his eternal glory in Christ Jesus enlighten your souls with his seven-fold light and establish you with his Spirit of freedom.

Before a First Holy Communion Class

It is useful on these occasions to use frequently the sorts of prayers that it is desirable the children know by heart. It is worth bearing in mind that whereas prayers using children's own language may by many be considered a good idea, these are the prayers the child will remember throughout his or her life, and if they are to be of use to the child when he or she is older, they will need to be in rather more mature language. A seven-year-old will easily understand and adapt.

By first Communion, a child should have learnt by heart at least the Our Father, the Hail Mary, the Glory be to the Father, an Act of Contrition (necessary, in any event, for the Sacrament of Penance) and perhaps one or two other prayers, such as that to their Guardian Angel.

HEAVENLY Father, we thank you for all that you have done for us. Above all we thank you for having given us your grace through the Sacrament of Baptism. We also thank you for our parents, for our brothers and sisters, and for our friends. We ask you now to help us prepare to receive our first Holy Communions. Help us to listen carefully and learn as much as we can about you today, so that we may truly become worthy to receive the Body and Blood of your Son Jesus Christ for the first time. Through the same Christ our Lord. Amen.

BEFORE A LECTURE

SHARPEN our minds, gracious inspiration of God, both speaker and listener, that we may truly understand what we speak and what we hear; may we profitably share knowlege and thus grow in wisdom the better to serve you and all humanity. Through Christ our Lord. Amen.

THE LECTURER OR TEACHER, FOR HIM OR HERSELF

St Anselm

GRANT me, O Lord, an eloquence that is both humble and wise; let me not be self-important, or think myself better than my fellows. By the inspiration of your Holy Spirit, put into my mouth words that console, that build up and exhort; so I may encourage by word and example the good to be better and those who are wandering to return to the narrow way. May the words which you have given your servant be as sharp spears and burning arrows to penetrate and inflame the minds of my hearers to respect and love you. Amen.

FOR CLERGY

FOR A PRIEST, BEFORE HEARING CONFESSIONS

Enchiridion

GRANT me, O Lord, the help of your wisdom, that I may know how to judge your people in justice, and your poor in right judgement. Help me to use the keys of the kingdom of heaven rightly, that I should open heaven to none to whom it should be closed, nor close it to whom it should be open. May my intentions be pure, my zeal sincere, my charity patient, and my labour fruitful.

May I possess gentleness that is not weakness, acuteness that is not severity; may I never despise the poor nor cultivate the rich. May I bind up sweetly the wounds of sin, ask questions prudently and give advice wisely.

May I be skilful in drawing back sinners from evil, and thorough in confirming the virtuous in good, to the making of greater effort; in my answers, grant me maturity; in my advice, rectitude; in doubtful matters, grant me light; in difficult, wisdom; let me not be distracted by useless chatter, nor let me be contaminated by evil.

May I save the souls of others, but not lose my own. Amen.

AFTER HEARING CONFESSIONS

LORD Jesus Christ, Son of the living God, receive this work of my ministry with the same all-embracing love with which you received and forgave the penitent Mary Magdalene and all other sinners who have fled to your tender arms. Be the perfecter of all that lacks in my kindness or zeal; and now I commend to your most Sacred Heart those whose confessions I have heard, and I beg that you preserve in them that grace which they have received from you today, that they may not fall again into those sins which have been forgiven them. May they and I come one day into your presence where you live and reign with God the Father and the Holy Spirit, one God for ever and ever. Amen.

Preparing a Homily

COME, Holy Spirit, and inspire my poor mind to understand your holy Word; do not let my prejudices, pride, or ill-formed opinions stand in the way of the truth that our Lord Jesus Christ came to proclaim; may my words and my whole life be a witness to that same Gospel that they may move others to repentance, to spiritual joy and ultimately to life in your kingdom where your live and reign for ever and ever. Amen.

After the 11th-Century Benedictional of Canterbury

O GOD, who have set the pastors of your Church as a lamp on a stand, and command that their light shine before people, and above all those in the household of God, grant me grace that I may enlighten those to whom I must preach, helping them to put on goodness and the armour of God. May the staff of courage be in my grasp to guide them through life; let my heart be full of wisdom, my speech be full of prudence that my life as well as my words may reflect that truth you sent your Son to teach us. Through the same Christ our Lord. Amen.

Visiting Homes

Missal of Robert of Jumièges

ALMIGHTY and merciful God, whose grace has given us the order of priesthood that service may be done in your name, and prayer made to you, we ask that you may visit those whom we visit today, and bless those whom we bless. May the merits of the saints go with us as we visit the homes of our parishioners, and may all evil be banished by the setting of your holy angel at the threshold.

Gelasian Sacramentary

MAY the peaceful light of your fatherly gaze enlighten this home. May the fulness of your blessing come upon all who live here, that while they live here safe and sound in this house which human hands have made, their hearts too may be your home. Amen.

FAMILIES

❦

A Newborn Child

A reading from the holy Gospel according to Luke.   18:15–16

THE people brought children to Jesus, that he might touch them. When the disciples saw this, they rebuked them. But Jesus, calling them together, said: Let the children come to me, and do not forbid them, for of such is the kingdom of God.

BLESSED be God the Father of our Lord Jesus Christ! Almighty God we praise and thank you for once more repeating your miracle of creation, and bringing this newborn child safely into the world. May he/she grow strong and healthy, wise and happy, and above all, holy.

Mother Mary, watch over this child. And we greet his/her Guardian Angel. We place this child in your loving care, to keep him/her from sin all his/her life. We pray also for the parents, N. and N. May their joy in this child never grow less: may they be good parents: friends as well as adults. May they never fail to set good example, so that we all, parents and child may come to your heavenly kingdom.

May almighty God bless this child and his/her parents; Father, Son ✠ and Holy Spirit. Amen.

A Bereavement

A reading from the holy Gospel according to John.   11:17

JESUS came to Bethany and found that his friend Lazarus had been four days already in the grave. Bethany was near Jerusalem, about two miles away. Many of the Jews had come to Martha and Mary, to comfort them concerning their brother. Martha therefore, as soon as she heard that Jesus had come, went to meet him, but Mary sat at home. And Martha said to Jesus: Lord, if you had been here, my brother would not have died. But I also know that whatever you ask of God, God will grant you. Jesus said to her: Your brother shall rise again. Martha said to him: I know that he shall rise again, at the resurrection on the last day. Jesus said to her: I am the resurrection and the life: he that believes in me, although he is dead, shall live, and every one that lives and believes in me shall never die. Do you believe this? She said to him: Yes, Lord, I believe that you are Christ, the Son of the living God, who has come into this world.

Let us pray.

L ORD Jesus Christ, son of the living God, hear our prayers in our sorrow at the death of N. Though we may be tempted to say, with Martha, Lord if you had been here, N. would not have died, grant us also her faith in you, the resurrection and the life. And as you raised Lazarus from the dead, so strengthen our belief that you will raise N. to life also, at the resurrection on the last day, when you make all things new, and the world of pain, illness and bereavement will be past. Strengthen our faith, we pray, that we will be joyfully reunited with N. in one communion of faith, life and love, never to be parted again. Who live and reign for ever and ever. Amen.

A Troublesome Family Member

The following reading will not be suitable in all circumstances.

A reading from the Gospel according to Luke. 15:12–32

J ESUS said: 'A certain man had two sons. And the younger of them said to his father: "Father, give me the share of the inheritance that will come to me [when you die]." And he divided his substance between them. And not many days after, the younger son, gathering everything together, went abroad into a far country, and there wasted his substance, living riotously. And after he had spent everything, there came a mighty famine in that country: and he began to be in need. So he went and joined one of the citizens of that country, who sent him into his farm to feed pigs. And he would happily have filled his belly with the husks the swine were eating, but no one gave him anything. And coming to himself, he said: "How many hired servants in my father's house have more than enough bread, and here I perish with hunger! I will arise and will go to my father and say to him: 'Father, I have sinned against heaven and before you. I am not worthy to be called your son: make me as one of your hired servants.'" And rising up, he went home to his father. And when he was still a long way off, his father saw him and was moved with compassion and running to him fell upon his neck and kissed him. And the son said to him: "Father, I have sinned against heaven and before you; I am not now worthy to be called your son." And the father said to his servants: "Bring quickly the best robe and put it on him: and put a ring on his hand and shoes on his feet. And bring here the fatted calf, and kill it: and let us eat and make merry: Because this my son was dead and is come to life again, was lost and is found." And they began to be merry. Meanwhile his elder son was in the field, and when he came and drew near to the house, he heard music and dancing. So he called one of the servants, and asked what these things meant. The servant said to him: 'Your brother has returned, and your father has killed the fatted calf, because he has received him safe and sound.' The brother was angry, and would not go in. His father therefore came out and began to entreat him. But he answered his father: 'Behold, for so many years I have served you, and I have never disobeyed your commands, and yet you have never given me a kid to make merry with my friends: But as soon as this son of yours is come, who has devoured his substance with harlots, you have killed the fatted calf for him.' But he said to him: 'Son, you are always with me, and all I have is yours. But it was fit that we should make merry and be glad, for this your brother was dead and has come to life again; he was lost, and is found.'

Let us pray.

HEAVENLY Father, loving and forgiving, we turn to you in our sorrow and perplexity. Send us your Holy Spirit that we may know what to do in this difficult solution. Help us to be loving, yet firm when it is needed, and give us infinite patience that N. may be able to feel the love we bear for him/her, and in time free himself/herself from what troubles him/her. Through Christ our Lord. Amen.

A TRAGEDY

A reading from the letter of St Paul to the Romans.   11:33–36

HOW rich are the depths of the wisdom and of the knowledge of God! How incomprehensible are his judgments, and how unsearchable his ways! For who has known the mind of the Lord? Or who has been his counsellor? Or who has given to him, or lent to him? For of him, and by him, and in him, are all things: to him be glory for ever. Amen.

Let us pray.

IN our perplexity, anxiety and sorrow, Lord God, we turn to you, the source of everything that is. We cannot pretend to understand your ways nor know the reasons for things being as they are. But we do know that you have a purpose for every one of our lives, and can bring good out of everything that befalls us. Help us to understand the reason for this sad circumstance; give us your Holy Spirit as our unfailing guide and comfort in the difficult times that may lie ahead, and enfold us in the pierced heart of your beloved Son for ever. Amen.

FOR THE SICK

On Receiving an Unfavourable Diagnosis

A reading from the letter to the Hebrews. 4:14–16, 5:7–8

HAVING therefore a great high priest that has passed into the heavens, Jesus the Son of God, let us hold fast to our confession [of faith]. For we have not a high priest who cannot have compassion on our infirmities, but one who has been tempted in all things as we are, but without sin. Let us go therefore with confidence to the throne of grace: that we may obtain mercy and find grace in the times we need it. For Jesus, in the days of his flesh, with a strong cry and tears, offered up prayers and supplications to the one that was able to save him from death, and was heard for his reverence. And whereas indeed he was the Son of God, he learned obedience by the things which he suffered, and being consummated, he became, to all that obey him, the cause of eternal salvation.

Let us pray.

O LORD Jesus Christ, the only doctor of our souls, create for us a pure heart and renew a right spirit within us. Bind up the wounds of our body and soul; repair that sacred image in which we were created, and which is now damaged by our sins and by our illness. Help us to understand that it is by bodily affliction that you seek to repair what is damaged within us, and by troubles in this world that you prepare us for eternal joys in the world to come. By the cup of sorrow which you drank for us, and by that weary path you trod, grant that we may accept your most holy will in all things and cheerfully follow you along the path where you have gone before, who live and reign for ever and ever. Amen.

May the most holy, adorable and wise will of God be done in all things, and in me. Amen.

In Great Pain

A reading from the prophet Isaiah.   53:3–5

HE was despised, and the most abject of men, a man of sorrows, and acquainted with infirmity: and his look was as it were hidden and despised, so we did not esteem him. But surely he has borne our infirmities and carried our sorrows: and we have thought him as like a leper, and as one struck by God and afflicted. But he was wounded for our iniquities, he was bruised for our sins: the chastisement of our peace was on him, and by his bruises we are healed.

Let us pray.

LORD Jesus Christ, who were willing to bear sorrows, agony, passion and death for the salvation of the world, and who called on us to take up our crosses and follow you: grant that we might bear our afflictions with patience for your sake, so that by sharing in your cross on earth we may share in your victory in heaven. Who live and reign for ever and ever. Amen.

DEAR Lord, as your hands were extended on the cross for the salvation of the world, I accept this suffering from your loving hands as a means to my own salvation and the forgiveness of my sins. May my suffering make me more like you.

O JESUS, good Samaritan, who poured into our wounds the sharp wine of affliction to wash away our sins, and sweet oil to take away the sting with your comfort, look upon your servant who is suffering, and now, if it be your will and for his/her good, relieve his/her bitterness and pain with the gift of your consolation, who live and reign for ever and ever. Amen.

ALMIGHTY God, who sent an angel to comfort your beloved Son in his passion, send your strength and help to this servant of yours now suffering and distressed. Through the same Christ our Lord. Amen.

For the Family of a Sick Person

A reading from the holy Gospel according to Luke. 7:1–10

JESUS entered into Capharnaum; there, a certain centurion had a servant, dear to him, who was sick and ready to die. And when the centurion heard of Jesus, he sent the elders of the Jews to him, desiring him to come and heal his servant. And when they came to Jesus, they beseeched him earnestly, saying to him: 'He is worthy that you should do this for him, for he loves our nation: and he has built us a synagogue.' So Jesus went with them. And when he was not far from the house, the centurion sent his friends to him, saying: 'Lord, do not trouble yourself; for I am not worthy that you should enter under my roof. This is why I did not think myself worthy to come to you: but only say the word, and my servant shall be healed. For I also am a man subject to authority, having soldiers under me: I say to one, "Go," and he goes, and to another, "Come," and he comes; and to my servant, "Do this," and he does it.' When Jesus heard this, he marvelled, and turning about to the multitude that followed him, he said: 'Truly I say to you: I have not found such great faith, not even in Israel.'

Let us pray.

LORD Jesus Christ, he/she whom you and we love is sick. We believe that you are the Son of God and can do all things. If it be your will, we pray that you heal N. from all his/her infirmities and restore him/her to us. Nonetheless, let it be according to your most holy will, who live and reign for ever and ever. Amen.

LORD, we pray that we may have the strength to bring good out of evil in this situation. May this adversity draw us together more strongly and fortify our love and concern for each other. May all pull their weight as is possible for them so that, if it be humanly possible, our practical love for N. who is sick may result in his/her healing. Through Christ our Lord. Amen.

For Those who Care for the Sick

LET us pray for all those dedicated to the care of N., (especially N. &c). O Lord, the true physician of both soul and body, who healed the sick, and cured the lame, we beg that you guide the hands that heal and the hearts that care; lend them your almighty strength and patience that their labour undertaken in love may not exhaust them in body or soul; may this illness teach us all, and shape us all into your own image, that those who are sick may see your face in those who care, and those who care may see your face in those who suffer, who live and reign for ever and ever. Amen.

A Blessing for Medicine

O LORD, whose almighty healing power is principally exercised through human acts and physical matter, as when your Son anointed the eyes of the blind man with spittle and clay that his sight might be restored, we ask you to bless ✠ these material things dedicated to N.'s healing (or alleviation of pain). Through the same Christ our Lord. Amen.

The Terminally Ill

A reading from the second letter of St Paul to Timothy.   4:6–8

I AM now ready to be sacrificed: and the time of my dissolution is at hand. I have fought the good fight: I have finished my race: I have kept the faith. As to the rest, there is laid up for me a crown of justice which the Lord, the just judge, will give to me on that day: and not only to me, but to all those that await his coming.

and/or

A reading from the book of Job.   19:25–27

I KNOW that my Redeemer lives, and that on the last day I shall rise again. And I shall be clothed again with my skin, and in my flesh I will see my God. I myself shall see him, and my eyes shall behold him, and not another: this my hope is laid up in my heart.

Let us pray.

S INCE it is your will, Lord, that all living things must one day return to you, give us the grace to use well such time we have before you call us to yourself. May we die at peace with you and with all those we know; may our sins and imperfections all be forgiven and washed clean in your Son's precious blood. Grant us inward tranquillity and docility; may our passing be calm and holy, fortified by your holy Sacraments and the prayers of your holy Church. May we not be a burden on those whom we love, but may whatever indignities or suffering we must bear win many blessings for our dear ones, offering our pains as we do in union with your beloved Son's passion and death, who lives and reigns with you and the Holy Spirit, God for ever and ever. Amen.

Mental Illness

A reading from the second letter of St Paul to the Corinthians.   1:3–7

B LESSED be the God and Father of our Lord Jesus Christ, the Father of mercies, and the God of all comfort, who comforts us in all our tribulation, that we also may be able to comfort those who are in any distress, by the encouragement with which we also are encouraged by God. For as the sufferings of Christ abound in us, so also by Christ does our comfort abound. Now if we are in tribulation, it is for your encouragement and salvation: if we are being comforted, it is for your consolation: if we are being encouraged, it is for your encouragement and salvation, which works when you patiently endure the same sufferings which we also suffer. Our hope for you is steadfast: knowing that as you are partakers of suffering, so shall you be also of consolation.

and/or

This other reading is intended to help the suffering person see his/her role as contributing to the salvation of the world, when offered together with the sufferings of Christ. It sometimes helps to identify a particular intention for which the sufferer can offer his/her distress. This can give the seemingly pointless suffering meaning to the sufferer, thus making it more bearable.

A reading from the letter of St Paul to the Colossians.   1:12–27

I GIVE thanks to God the Father, who has made us worthy to be partakers of the lot of the saints in light, who has delivered us from the power of darkness, and has translated us into the kingdom of the Son whom he loves. In him we have redemption through his blood, the remission of sins; he is the image of the invisible God, the firstborn of every creature: in him were all things created in heaven and on earth, visible and invisible, whether thrones, or dominations, or principalities, or powers: all things were created by him and in him. And he is before all, and by him all things consist. And he is the head of the body, the church, who is the beginning, the firstborn from the dead; that in all things he may hold the primacy: Because in him, it has well pleased the Father that all fullness should dwell, and through him to reconcile all things to himself, making peace by the blood of his cross, both the things that are on earth, and the things that are in heaven. And you, whereas you were once alienated and enemies in mind and in evil works, now he has reconciled you in the body of his flesh through death, to present you holy and unspotted, and blameless before him. So continue in the faith, grounded and settled, and immoveable from the hope of the gospel which you have heard, which is preached in all creation that is under heaven, and of which I, Paul, am made a minister. So I now rejoice in my sufferings for you, because I can fill up in my flesh those things that are lacking to the sufferings of Christ for his body, which is the church. Of the church I am made a minister according to the dispensation of God which is given to me for you, that I may fulfil the word of God, the mystery which has been hidden from ages and generations, but now is manifested to his saints, to whom God would make known the riches of the glory of this mystery among the nations, which is Christ, in you the hope of glory.

Let us pray.

L ORD God, who love us with an unutterable love, be our light in darkness, and our comfort in tribulation. We pray for patience and endurance in this distressing illness; help us to understand the role you have asked us to share in the salvation of ourselves and of others in this suffering.

L ORD Jesus, whose distress of mind caused you to sweat blood in the garden of Gethsamene, whose head was tormented by the crown of thorns, and who bore your cross to Calvary, help us to bear what must be borne with patience. We pray that you take this cup of suffering from us; nonetheless let it be according to your most holy will. Send your holy angels to be our comfort in this distress of mind; for your name's sake. Amen.

FAMILY OF THOSE WITH A MENTAL ILLNESS

A reading from the holy Gospel according to Mark. 11:22–25

J ESUS said to his disciples: 'Have faith in God. Truly I say to you that whoever shall say to this mountain, "Be removed and be cast into the sea," and shall not falter in his heart but believe that whatever he asks shall be done, it shall be done for him. Therefore I say to you, whatsoever you ask when you pray, believe that you shall receive all things; and they will come to you.'

Let us pray.

A LMIGHTY Father, we pray for N., suffering in mind at this time. Be his/her strength, comfort and close companion in his/her trial. We believe that you are all-powerful, and can do whatever you will; strengthen our faith that you desire to heal N., and enable us to do whatever we can towards that same end. Help us to be patient and understanding at all times, and give us strength to respond appropriately in each different situation that may confront us. May our love never falter, for you or for N. We ask this through Christ our Lord. Amen.

WITH A SICK CHILD

A reading from the holy Gospel according to Mark.   6:53–56

W HEN Jesus and his disciples had crossed over the sea, they came to the land of Genesareth, and tied up. And when they got out of the boat, immediately they were recognized. And hurrying through that whole country, the people began to carry in beds those that were sick, to wherever they heard he was. So wherever he entered, into towns or into villages or cities, they laid the sick in the streets, and begged him that they might touch only the hem of his garment: and whoever touched him was healed.

Or

A reading from the holy Gospel according to Luke.   8:41, 42, 50

T HERE came a man whose name was Jairus: and he was a ruler of the synagogue. He fell down at the feet of Jesus, begging him to come to his house, for he had an only daughter, almost twelve years old, who was dying. And Jesus answered the father of the girl: Fear not. Only have faith: and she shall be safe.

Let us pray.

L ORD Jesus Christ, we know from the Gospels that you healed the sick, and we believe that you can do so now. Hear our prayers for N. who is ill; if it is your will, we ask that he/she be made well again. Keep him/her cheerful and happy, and grant him/her the love and support of all his/her friends and family. Bless all the doctors and nurses who do good in trying to heal people, and make them truly skilful and kind. We ask you to heal all sick people wherever they may be. Amen.

Family with a Sick Child

A reading from the holy Gospel according to Luke.   7:1–10

JESUS entered into Capharnaum; there, a certain centurion had a servant, dear to him, who was sick and ready to die. And when the centurion heard of Jesus, he sent the elders of the Jews to him, desiring him to come and heal his servant. And when they came to Jesus, they beseeched him earnestly, saying to him: 'He is worthy that you should do this for him, for he loves our nation: and he has built us a synagogue.'

So Jesus went with them. And when he was not far from the house, the centurion sent his friends to him, saying: 'Lord, do not trouble yourself; for I am not worthy that you should enter under my roof. This is why I did not think myself worthy to come to you: but only say the word, and my servant shall be healed. For I also am a man subject to authority, having soldiers under me: I say to one, "Go," and he goes, and to another, "Come," and he comes; and to my servant, "Do this," and he does it.'

When Jesus heard this, he marvelled, and turning about to the multitude that followed him, he said: 'Truly I say to you: I have not found such great faith, not even in Israel.' And when those who were sent returned to the house, they found the servant who had been sick was healed.

ALMIGHTY Father, who healed the sick not only for their own sake, but for the sake of those who loved them, hear our prayers for N. whom we love and whom now we entrust to your fatherly care. If it be your will, dear Lord, heal and restore him/her to us with all speed. Give us strength to provide all the love and care that N. needs, and grant to doctors and nurses the skill they need to bring healing to the one we love. Through Christ our Lord. Amen.

141

DISABILITIES

At Risk of the Loss of Sight

A reading from the holy Gospel according to Mark.   10:46–52

JESUS came to Jericho; and as he went out of Jericho with his disciples and a very great crowd, Bartimeus the blind man, the son of Timeus, sat by the wayside begging. When he had heard that it was Jesus of Nazareth passing, he began to cry out and to say: 'Jesus son of David, have mercy on me.' And many people rebuked him, telling him to hold his peace, but he cried a great deal more: 'Son of David, have mercy on me.' And Jesus, standing still, commanded that he be called. So they called the blind man, saying to him: 'Be happy: get up; he is calling you.' Casting off his garment, he leapt up, and came to him. And Jesus said to him: 'What do you want me to do for you?' And the blind man said to him: 'Rabboni, that I may see.' And Jesus said to him: 'Go your way, your faith has made you whole.' And immediately he saw, and followed him on the road.

Let us pray.

LORD God, at this anxious time we call for your light, in more senses than one. We ask in the first place for calmness, understanding and that peace which the world cannot give. And we also ask that if it be your will, the light of this world may be fully restored to your servant. But if it cannot be, we ask an increase of grace and of heavenly light, that N. may see more clearly into those things of the spirit that really matter. We pray that friends and family may rally round; that quality of life may be experienced to the full, and ultimately that we may all come to see you face to face in heaven, where you live and reign for ever and ever. Amen.

On the Loss of Sight

A reading from the book of Job.   19:25–27

I KNOW that my Redeemer lives, and that on the last day I shall rise again. And I shall be clothed again with my skin, and in my flesh I will see my God. I myself shall see him, and my eyes shall behold him, and not another: this my hope is laid up in my heart.

Let us pray.

LORD God, since it is your will that your servant N. should lose his/her sight, we ask that he/she may look on you with ever more perceptive inward eyes of faith; may he/she look now on the kingdom of heaven with unclouded vision, and have faith that one day he/she may, in his/her flesh, look upon his/her Redeemer, our Lord Jesus Christ who lives and reigns with you and the Holy Spirit, one God for ever and ever. Amen.

GIVE us patience, Lord, in this time of trial. Help us to understand what has happened, and see it as part of the sad fate of the world which you came to free us from. In the difficult days ahead, help us to cope, to be inwardly strong and determined not to let this beat us. Make us generous and patient with those who don't understand how we feel, or who are insensitive, or unhelpful. Give us the earthly help we need; the love of friends and family, and the co-operation of public services; but above all give us yourself, and your heavenly wisdom, that one day we may find that this earthly tragedy may prove to have been a heavenly blessing. May your grace, building on our patient endurance, win us the crown of everlasting life. Amen.

LOSS OF HEARING

A reading from the holy Gospel according to Mark. 7:32–37

THEY brought to Jesus someone who was deaf and dumb; and they asked him to lay his hand upon him. So taking him apart from the crowd, he put his fingers into his ears, and with spittle he touched his tongue. And looking up to heaven, he groaned, and said to him: Ephpheta, which is, Be opened. And immediately his ears were opened, and the ligament of his tongue was loosened, and he spoke clearly. And he charged them that they should tell no one. But the more he warned them, so much the more did they speak of it. And so much the more did they wonder, saying: He has done all things well; he has made the deaf hear, and the dumb speak.

Let us pray.

BE with us, Lord, at this difficult time. Grant us patience and faith to cope with what we are going through. Grant skill and insight to those engaged in treating this condition, and if it be your will, we pray for a restoration of hearing. If this is not possible, dear Lord, we pray for the ability to accept what must be and to see it with the eyes of faith as coming from your loving providence, since you desire our salvation above all else, and who live and reign for ever and ever. Amen.

At Risk of the Loss of Mobility

A reading from the holy Gospel according to Luke.   5:17–26

IT came to pass on a certain day, as Jesus sat teaching, that there were also Pharisees and doctors of the law sitting by, who had come from every town of Galilee, and Judea and Jerusalem: and the power of the Lord was present to heal them. Then some men carried in a bed a man who was paralysed: and they sought for means to bring him in, and to lay him before Jesus. And when they could not find a way to bring him in because of the crowd, they went up on the roof, and let him down through the tiles with his bed into the midst before Jesus. When he saw his faith, he said: 'Man, your sins are forgiven.' And the scribes and Pharisees began to think, saying: 'Who is this who speaks blasphemy? Who can forgive sins, but God alone?' When Jesus knew their thoughts, he said to them: 'What is it you think in your hearts? Which is easier to say, "Your sins are forgiven," or "Arise and walk?" But that you may know that the Son of man has power on earth to forgive sins,' (he said to the paralysed man,) 'I say to you, Arise, take up your bed, and go to your house.' And immediately rising up before them, he took up the bed on which he lay; and he went away to his own house, glorifying God. And all were astonished; and they glorified God. And they were filled with fear, saying: 'We have seen wonderful things today.'

Let us pray.

ALMIGHTY God, we know that by your power you can do all things; strengthen, we pray, our infirmity and grant us your healing strength that we may run in the way of your commands, and once more with our whole body serve you gladly. But if it be your will that we suffer disability, grant us the help we need to bear it gracefully: both that human assistance that we may need, but also your gifts of patience, tolerance and faith, and that peace which the world cannot give. Through Christ our Lord. Amen.

On the Loss of Mobility

A reading from the prophet Isaiah. 35:3–7

STRENGTHEN the feeble hands, and make firm the weak knees. Say to the fainthearted: Take courage, and fear not: behold your God will bring the reward of recompense: God himself will come and will save you. Then shall the eyes of the blind be opened, and the ears of the deaf shall be unstopped. Then shall the lame man leap as a deer, and the tongue of the dumb shall be free: for waters shall break forth in the desert, and streams in the wilderness. And that which was dry land shall become a pool, and the thirsty land, springs of water.

Let us pray.

LORD God, our heavenly physician, we beg your gracious assistance in our needs. Strengthen our faith in your divine providence, and help us to understand how we may serve you best in this situation. We believe strongly that despite whatever must be here on earth, that one day we shall stand before you once more in all our health and strength and praise you for your goodness. May whatever inconveniences and indignities attend this disability prepare and further the cause of our redemption, forgive us our sins, help us grow in holiness, and help us one day see you face to face. Through Christ our Lord. Amen.

Children with Learning Difficulties

A reading from the holy Gospel according to Luke. 18:15–17

THE people brought children to Jesus, that he might touch them. When the disciples saw this, they rebuked them. But Jesus, calling them together, said: 'Let the children come to me, and do not forbid them, for of such is the kingdom of God. Truly, I say to you: Whoever does not receive the kingdom of God like a child shall not enter into it.'

Let us pray.

LORD God, hear our prayers for N. We know that the children and the childlike are especially dear to you, and we rejoice that this means that N. is more dear to you even than other children. May he/she most importantly continue to grow in your love, and also in our love. Help us all to do all the right things to enable him/her to reach his/her full potential in life, and grant him/her your especial protection for the times when things get tough. May we all one day see and understand this difficulty in the context of your blessed providence, for we know that you love and care for us all with a never-failing love. Through Christ our Lord. Amen.

Adults with Special Needs
Such as Mental Handicap or Learning Difficulties

A reading from the letter of St Paul to the Romans.   11:33–36

O THE depth of the riches of the wisdom and of the knowledge of God! How incomprehensible are his judgments, and how unsearchable his ways! For who has known the mind of the Lord? Or who has been his counsellor? Or who has first given to him that he might be repaid? For from him, and by him, and in him, are all things: to him be glory for ever. Amen.

Another translation

O HOW wise and how knowledgeable God is! How hard it is to understand his decisions, and how deep is his intelligence! Who can understand what the Lord is thinking? Who can give him advice? Who can even lend him anything to get it back again? Because all things come from him, he made everything, and keeps everything going; we praise him for ever. Amen.

Let us pray.

L ORD God, whose wisdom and providence guides us from day to day with your mighty power, hear our prayer for N. Watch over him/her with your fatherly care, and grant him/her your protection and love throughout life. Grant him/her wisdom in the things that really matter; goodness, holiness and love. Through Christ our Lord. Amen.

and/or

L ORD God and Father, we thank you for all the good things you have done for us; we thank you for loving us, and sending us Jesus your

Son to love us even more. Help us to be clever in the really important things of life, and give us help when we really need it. Through Christ our Lord. Amen.

A Child with Downs Syndrome

A reading from the holy Gospel according to Luke.   18:15–17

THE people brought children to Jesus, that he might touch them. When the disciples saw this, they rebuked them. But Jesus, calling them together, said: Let the children come to me, and do not forbid them, for of such is the kingdom of God. Truly, I say to you: Whoever does not receive the kingdom of God like a child shall not enter into it.

Let us pray.

HEAVENLY Father, whose ways are unsearchable and whose foolishness is wiser than earthly wisdom, we commend to your Sacred Heart this child N. whom your Providence has given to us to nurture and love, and who we know will bring such blessing to our home. Help us to be wise and strong in all the right ways; help us and all around us to cope with whatever difficulties may come. May we, too, learn love and simplicity from N., without which we cannot enter the kingdom of heaven, and thus, learning from each other, may we all one day stand before you and know you in all wisdom and truth. Through Christ our Lord. Amen.

THE INTERNET

PRAYER BEFORE USING THE INTERNET

ALMIGHTY and eternal God, who created us in your image and commanded us to seek after all that is good, true and beautiful, especially in the divine person of your only-begotten Son, our Lord Jesus Christ: grant, we pray, that, through the intercession of Saint Isidore, Bishop and Doctor, during our journeys through the internet we will direct our hands and eyes only to that which is pleasing to you and treat with charity and patience all those souls whom we encounter. Through Christ our Lord. Amen.

Fr John Zuhlsdorf, alt.

ANOTHER PRAYER

DIRECT our eyes and our hands, Lord God, to the doing of your will. Let us fall into no sin against charity or chastity today or ever. Through Christ our Lord. Amen.

PETS

A New Pet

Let us pray.

ALMIGHTY God, who gave your servant Tobias a dog as a comfort and protection on his journey, we thank you for the gift of N. May we treat him/her humanely and responsibly, and may he/she be a comfort and a companion to us in our journey through life. Through Christ our Lord. Amen.

A Sick Animal

Let us pray.

HEAVENLY Father, who see even the fall of a sparrow, we ask your healing for N. who is sick; if it be your will, restore him/her to health for our comfort and to your greater glory. Through Christ our Lord. Amen.

A Pet Funeral

Let us pray.

LORD our God, who love everything that you have made, we thank you for the blessings you have given us during the life of N., and for the happiness he/she has given us. With sorrow, but with trust in your merciful goodness, we return his/her body to the earth from which it came. Grant to us a speedy release from our sorrow, and help us to find our comfort in you, the source of all true love. Through Christ our Lord. Amen.

Service for the Blessing of Pets
SEE P. 172

PART IV

OCCASIONAL
SERVICES

THE GREAT LITANY

Lord, have mercy,	**Lord, have mercy.**
Christ, have mercy,	**Christ, have mercy.**
Lord, have mercy,	**Lord, have mercy.**
God the Father of heaven,	**have mercy on us.**
God the Son, Redeemer of the world,	**have mercy on us.**
God the Holy Spirit,	**have mercy on us.**
Holy Trinity, one God,	**have mercy on us.**
Holy Mary,	**pray for us.**
Holy Mother of God,	**pray for us.**
Holy Virgin of virgins,	**pray for us.**
Saints Michael, Gabriel and Raphael,	**pray for us.**
All holy Angels,	**pray for us.**
Holy Abraham,	**pray for us.**
Holy Moses,	**pray for us.**
Holy Elijah,	**pray for us.**
Saint John the Baptist,	**pray for us.**
Saint Joseph,	**pray for us.**
All holy patriarchs and prophets,	**pray for us.**
Saints Peter and Paul,	**pray for us.**
Saint Andrew,	**pray for us.**
Saints James and John,	**pray for us.**
Saint Thomas,	**pray for us.**
Saint Matthew,	**pray for us.**
All holy Apostles,	**pray for us.**
Saint Luke,	**pray for us.**
Saint Mark,	**pray for us.**
Saint Barnabas,	**pray for us.**
Saint Mary Magdalen,	**pray for us.**
All holy disciples of the Lord,	**pray for us.**

Saint Stephen,	**pray for us.**
Saint Ignatius of Antioch,	**pray for us.**
Saint Polycarp,	**pray for us.**
Saint Justin,	**pray for us.**
Saint Laurence,	**pray for us.**
Saint Cyprian,	**pray for us.**
Saint Boniface,	**pray for us.**
Saint Stanislaus,	**pray for us.**
Saint Thomas Becket,	**pray for us.**
Saints John Fisher and Thomas More,	**pray for us.**
Saint Paul Miki,	**pray for us.**
Saints John de Brébeuf and Isaac Jogues,	**pray for us.**
Saint Peter Chanel,	**pray for us.**
Saint Charles Lwanga,	**pray for us.**
Saints Perpetua and Felicity,	**pray for us.**
Saint Agnes,	**pray for us.**
Saint Maria Goretti,	**pray for us.**
All holy martyrs,	**pray for us.**
Saints Leo and Gregory,	**pray for us.**
Saint Ambrose,	**pray for us.**
Saint Jerome,	**pray for us.**
Saint Augustine,	**pray for us.**
Saint Athanasius,	**pray for us.**
Saints Basil and Gregory Nazienzen,	**pray for us.**
Saint John Chrysostom,	**pray for us.**
Saint Martin,	**pray for us.**
Saint Patrick,	**pray for us.**
Saints Cyril and Methodius,	**pray for us.**
Saint Charles Borromeo,	**pray for us.**
Saint Francis de Sales,	**pray for us.**
Saint Pius the Tenth,	**pray for us.**
Saint Anthony,	**pray for us.**
Saint Benedict,	**pray for us.**
Saint Bernard,	**pray for us.**
Saints Francis and Dominic,	**pray for us.**
Saint Thomas Aquinas,	**pray for us.**
Saint Ignatius of Loyola,	**pray for us.**
Saint Francis Xavier,	**pray for us.**
Saint Vincent de Paul,	**pray for us.**

Saint John Mary Vianney,	**pray for us.**
Saint John Bosco,	**pray for us.**
Saint Catherine of Siena,	**pray for us.**
Saint Teresa of Avila,	**pray for us.**
Saint Rose of Lima,	**pray for us.**
Saint Louis,	**pray for us.**
Saint Monica,	**pray for us.**
Saint Elizabeth of Hungary,	**pray for us.**
Saint Teresa of Kolkata,	**pray for us.**
(Other saints and patrons)	
Blessed John Henry Newman,	**pray for us.**
All holy saints of God,	**pray for us.**
Be merciful:	**Lord, deliver us.**
From all evil,	**Lord, deliver us.**
From all sin,	**Lord, deliver us.**
From the snares of the devil,	**Lord, deliver us.**
From anger, hate and all ill-will,	**Lord, deliver us.**
From everlasting death,	**Lord, deliver us.**
By your incarnation,	**Lord, deliver us.**
By your nativity,	**Lord, deliver us.**
By your baptism and holy fast,	**Lord, deliver us.**
By your cross and passion,	**Lord, deliver us.**
By your death and burial,	**Lord, deliver us.**
By your holy resurrection,	**Lord, deliver us.**
By your wonderful ascension,	**Lord, deliver us.**
By your pouring out of the Holy Spirit,	**Lord, deliver us.**
By your glorious second coming,	**Lord, deliver us.**
Christ, Son of the living God,	**have mercy on us.**
Who came into this world,	**have mercy on us.**
Who hung upon the cross,	**have mercy on us.**
Who accepted death for our sakes,	**have mercy on us.**
Who lay buried in the tomb,	**have mercy on us.**
Who arose from death,	**have mercy on us.**
Who ascended to heaven,	**have mercy on us.**
Who sent the Holy Spirit upon the Apostles,	**have mercy on us.**
Who are seated at the right hand of the Father,	**have mercy on us.**
Who will come to judge the living and the dead,	**have mercy on us.**

That you might spare us,	**Hear us, Lord, we pray.**
That you might draw us to true repentance,	**Hear us, Lord, we pray.**
That you might confirm us in your holy service,	**Hear us, Lord, we pray.**
That you might grant all our benefactors eternal reward,	**Hear us, Lord, we pray.**
That you might grant us the fruits of the earth,	**Hear us, Lord, we pray.**
That you might be patient with us,	**Hear us, Lord, we pray.**
That you might lift our minds to heavenly things,	**Hear us, Lord, we pray.**
That you might free our souls, and those of our neighbours and benefactors from eternal damnation,	**Hear us, Lord, we pray.**
That you might give rest to all the faithful departed,	**Hear us, Lord, we pray.**
That you might keep the world from disease, famine and war,	**Hear us, Lord, we pray.**
That you might grant to all people peace and true concord,	**Hear us, Lord, we pray.**
That you might be pleased to govern and keep your holy Church,	**Hear us, Lord, we pray.**
That you might be pleased to keep the Pope and all in Holy Orders true in holy religion,	**Hear us, Lord, we pray.**
That you might grant unity to all who believe in Christ,	**Hear us, Lord, we pray.**
That you might lead all people to the light of the Gospel,	**Hear us, Lord, we pray.**
Lamb of God, you take away the sins of the world;	**have mercy on us.**
Lamb of God, you take away the sins of the world;	**have mercy on us.**
Lamb of God, you take away the sins of the world;	**have mercy on us.**

Christ, hear us.	**Christ, hear us.**
Christ, graciously hear us.	**Christ, graciously hear us.**
Lord, have mercy,	**Lord, have mercy.**
Christ, have mercy,	**Christ, have mercy.**
Lord, have mercy,	**Lord, have mercy.**

Let us pray.

O GOD, our refuge and strength, author of all holiness, hear the prayers of your holy Church, and grant what we faithfully ask. Through Christ our Lord. Amen.

RECEPTION OF A DIOCESAN BISHOP

This short service is the manner in which a diocesan bishop is formally received into a church within his own jurisdiction on the occasion of a visitation or other official business.

The bishop, in choir dress, is met at the door of the church by the parish priest (or rector of the church) wearing a cope, other clergy, and also the servers. The bishop is presented by the parish priest with a crucifix on a cushion to kiss, and is then given holy water, with which he blesses himself and sprinkles all present at the church's entrance.

The procession leads off to wherever the Blessed Sacrament is reserved. There may be a hymn, or the choir may sing Ecce Sacerdos Magnus, *or the organ simply play. The Bishop walks at the rear of the procession accompanied by the MC and preceded by the parish priest.*

At the place of reservation there should be a prie-dieu for the bishop. All genuflect and remain kneeling in prayer for a while. All rise with the bishop, and the procession goes to the sanctuary (if the Blessed Sacrament is reserved outside the sanctuary).

From the altar, the parish priest reads the collect for a bishop, as found in the Roman Missal on pp. 1306 and 1307.

This being done, the bishop addresses the people, and then prays the collect for the patron of the church. He blesses the people in the usual way, and then the parish priest dismisses them if there be no ceremony to follow directly.

This concludes the rite of reception. If Mass is to follow directly, the celebrant (priest or bishop) vests on the sanctuary. If the diocesan bishop is celebrating, it is customary to place seven candles on the altar. He may also have seven acolytes at the Mass, though for obvious reasons this is very rarely observed.

THE ADOPTION OF A CHILD

༄༅

A reading from the prophet Hosea. 11:1–4, 11

ISRAEL was a child, and I loved him: and I called my son out of Egypt ... And I was like a foster father to Ephraim, I carried them in my arms: and they did not know that I healed them. I will draw them with the cords of compassion, with the bands of love, and I will be to them as one that takes off the yoke on their jaws: and I will give them food that they might eat ... And they shall fly like a bird out of Egypt, and like a dove out of the land of the Assyrians: and I will place them in their own homes, says the Lord.

or

A reading from the prophet Isaiah. 43:1–7

THUS says the Lord that created you, O Jacob, and formed you, O Israel: Fear not, for I have redeemed you, and called you by your name: you are mine. When you shall pass through the waters, I will be with you, and the rivers shall not cover you: when you walk in the fire, you will not be burnt, and the flames shall not burn you: For I am the Lord your God, the Holy One of Israel, your Saviour: I have given Egypt for your ransom, Ethiopia and Saba for you. Since you are precious in my eyes, you are glorious: I have loved you, and I will give men for you, and people for your life. Fear not, for I am with you: I will bring your descendants from the east, and gather you from the west. I will say to the north: give up: and to the south: do not keep back: bring my sons from afar, and my daughters from the ends of the earth. And I have created for my glory every one that calls upon my name; I have formed him, and made him.

The celebrant addresses the parents:

Celebrant: Do you promise before God to nurture, protect and guide N. into adulthood?

Parents: **I do.**

Celebrant: Do you promise to help him/her grow spiritually, physically, emotionally, and academically?

Parents: **I do.**

Celebrant: Do you promise to bring N. up according to the law of Christ and his Church?

Parents: **I do**

Celebrant: Do you promise before God, to love N. to the best of your ability, as you would the child of your own body, to provide him/her with stability, affection, and appropriate discipline?

Parents: **I do.**

Should the child be old enough, he/she may also make this promise:

Celebrant: N., you see before you two people, N., and N., who desire to give you a home and share everything with you, such that you will truly become part of their family for ever.

Do you promise on your part to do all that you can to be a good son/daughter to them as long as they shall live?

Child: **I do.**

Let us pray.

ALMIGHTY Father, whose love for us your children exceeds anything we deserve or can even know, we thank you for the joy of this day. Bless the generosity of N. and N. who have opened their home and their lives to N. May their love for each other grow day by day. We ask for these parents abundant gifts of your Holy Spirit; above all holiness, strength, tolerance, wisdom and patience. For their new son/daughter, we beseech you for strong faith, a sense of security, courage, calmness, temperance and right judgement as they grow in wisdom and stature before you. May all gathered here be blessed in all they do. Through your only Son our Lord Jesus Christ, who lives and reigns with you and the Holy Spirit, one God for ever and ever. Amen.

MAY the power of the Father, the wisdom of the Son, the love of the Holy Spirit be with you, and may the grace of the holy and undivided Trinity be upon you now and for ever. Amen.

THE INSTITUTION OF A CANTOR
OR CHORISTER, OR PSALMIST

ANCIENT FORM

The Cantor is simply given the following charge:

SEE that what you sing with your mouth you believe with your heart, and may what you believe with your heart be revealed in what you do.

A LONGER VERSION

℣, Our help is in the name of the Lord.
℟. **Who made heaven and earth.**
℣. The Lord be with you.
℟. **And with your spirit.**

Let us pray.

ALMIGHTY God, who conjoined in your beloved servant David mighty faith with surpassing beauty of voice, grant that your servants who fulfil the office of cantor in this assembly may exercise their gifts with sincerity and becoming humility to the honour of your name. Through Christ our Lord. Amen.

Each cantor should approach the celebrant, and kneel. He or she may then be given some symbol of the office (such as a book of Psalms) with the words:

SEE that what you sing with your mouth you believe with your heart, and may what you believe with your heart be revealed in what you do.

When all have been invested with the symbol of office, the celebrant says:

And may the peace and blessing of Almighty God, Father, Son ✠ and Holy Spirit, come down upon you and remain with you for ever.

ALTAR SERVERS

Enrolment in the Guild of St Stephen

The ceremony may take place during Mass (preferably a Votive Mass of St Stephen, when permitted), after the homily.

Those servers to be enrolled are called forward either as a group or by name, and stand in front of the priest. The parish Master of Ceremonies presents the candidates.

MC: Let those who are called to the ministry of serving at the altar please come forward.

Celebrant: What do you ask of God's Church?

Servers: **The blessing of Almighty God and enrolment into the Guild of Saint Stephen for altar servers.**

Celebrant: Do you recommend their admission to the guild?

MC: Reverend Fathers and Parishioners of *(Parish)*, these young members of our parish have completed a probationary period of service at the altar of our church. They have shown themselves to be reverent in their actions, regular in their attendance and to have an understanding of the Mass and most importantly a love of the Lord Jesus whom they now seek to serve as members of the Guild.

Everyone sits—the candidates on seats prepared for them in the sanctuary. The priest addresses the candidates in these, or similar words:

DEAR servers, you have heard the recommendation made on your behalf by our Parish MC. Before you undertake this commitment may I remind you, and indeed all servers present that the worship of the Church is centred on the celebration of administration of the Sacraments. Those who are ordained for this are the Bishop, the Priest and the Deacon. But, from earliest times, the Church has called other Christians to assist at these services, principally to help the ordained ministers, but also to be at the service of the entire Christian Community. To be called to assist the Church in this manner is a privileged function and should be carried out to the best of one's ability. You must always try to serve in such a way to help everyone in the church to pray. Remember, always, the promises that you are about to make:

To serve regularly, at the times when you are asked,

To serve with care and reverence, and, above all,

To serve with understanding.

A good server is the one who not only knows what to do, but also understands why it is being done. Try to learn more about the worship of the Church, in which you are being called to participate in a privileged way.

All stand. The candidates kneel in front of the priest, and they may be given a lit candle to hold.

Celebrant: My dear people, let us pray for those who wish to be enrolled into the Guild of St Stephen. Let us ask God to bless them.

There is a pause for silent prayer.

HEAVENLY Father, bless ✠ these servers who have been chosen to be members of the Guild of St Stephen. Grant that they may be faithful in their service at your altar, and that they may grow in faith and love. We ask this through Christ our Lord. Amen.

Celebrant: Will you try to say the Guild prayer every day?

Servers: **I will, with the help of God.**

Celebrant: Will you promise to do your best to serve regularly, particularly when you are needed?

Servers: **I will, with the help of God.**

Celebrant: Will you promise to serve with care and reverence?

Servers: **I will, with the help of God.**

Celebrant: Will you try to understand what you are doing when you serve?

Servers: **I will, with the help of God.**

Celebrant: I now invite all enrolled members of the Guild to stand and join with those to be enrolled in making the Guild promise.

Servers: **I offer myself to God Almighty, to Blessed Mary, our Mother, and to our holy Patron, St Stephen, and I promise to do my best to serve regularly, with reverence and understanding, for the glory of God, the service of his Church, and my own eternal salvation.**

BLESSING OF THE MEDALS

Blessed are you, Lord of all creation. You have made us in your image and likeness, and placed us over all creation to use it for your glory. We ask you to bless ✠ these medals which your servers will wear as a sign of their service at your altar.

The medals are sprinkled with holy water.
In the name of the Father, and of the Son, and of the Holy Spirit. Amen.

The celebrant places a medal around the neck of each server, saying:

Priest: N. receive this medal as a token of your admission into the Guild of St Stephen; that, with the help of his prayers, you may lead a good and holy life.

Server: **Amen.**

The newly-enrolled servers may then sign the parish enrolment register.

Let us pray.

L ORD Jesus Christ, you came into this world to serve others, rather than to be served, and showed yourself to St Stephen in your glory at the right hand of the Father. We ask you to grant to your altar servers the faith of St Stephen, as they serve you in the Blessed Sacrament, till they too come to see you in your glory, who live and reign for ever and ever. Amen.

A SOLEMN COVENANT

TO FOLLOW A RETREAT

❧ ✦ ❧

This service is taken from The Methodist Worship Book, *and in that context is used by the entire congregation early each year. It seems a highly appropriate act to make after having completed a retreat, and in view of the probability that each retreatant has made a good general confession in the course of the retreat, the penitential rite has been omitted from this service.*

℣. The Lord be with you.
℟. And with your spirit.

GOD made a covenant with the people of Israel, calling them to be a holy nation, chosen to bear witness to his steadfast love by finding delight in the law.

The covenant was renewed in Jesus Christ our Lord, in his life, work, death and resurrection. In him all people may be set free from sin and its power, and united in love and obedience.

In this covenant, God promises us new life in Christ. For our part we promise to live no longer for ourselves but for God.

We meet, therefore, as generations have met before us, to renew the covenant which bound them and binds us to God.

Sisters and brothers in Christ, let us again accept our place within this covenant which God has made with us and with all who are called to be Christ's disciples.

This means that, by the help of the Holy Spirit, we accept God's purpose for us, and the call to love and serve God in all our life and work.

Christ has many services to be done: some are easy, others are difficult; some bring honour, others bring reproach; some are suitable to our natural inclinations and material interests, others are contrary to both; in some we may please Christ and please ourselves; in others we cannot please Christ except by denying ourselves. Yet the power to do all these things is given to us in Christ, who strengthens us.

Therefore let us make this covenant with God our own. Let us give ourselves to him, trusting in his promises and relying on his grace.

165

Eternal God, in your faithful and enduring love you call us to share in your gracious covenant in Jesus Christ. In obedience we hear and accept your commands; in love we seek to do your perfect will; with joy we offer ourselves anew to you. We are no longer our own but yours.

> I am no longer mine, but yours.
> Your will, not mine, be done in all things.
>> wherever you may place me,
>> in all that I do
>>> and in all that I may endure;
>> when there is work for me
>>> and when there is none;
>> when I am troubled
>>> and when I am at peace.
>
> Your will be done
>> when I am valued
>>> and when I am disregarded;
>> when I find fulfilment
>>> and when it is lacking;
>> when I have all things,
>>> and when I have nothing.
>
> I willingly offer
>> all I have and am
>> to serve you,
>>> as and where you choose.
>
> Glorious and blessed God,
>> Father, Son and Holy Spirit,
>>> you are mine and I am yours.
>> May it be so for ever.
> Let this covenant now made on earth
>> be fulfilled in heaven. Amen.

Taken from the Methodist Worship Book,
© 1999 Trustees for Methodist Church Purposes,
used by permission of Methodist Publishing House

CIVIC OCCASIONS

FOUNDATION STONES

A reading from the letter of St Paul to the Ephesians.   2:19–22

NOW therefore no more are you strangers and foreigners: but you are fellow citizens with the saints and the family of God, built upon the foundation of the apostles and prophets, Jesus Christ himself being the chief corner stone in whom all the building, being framed together, grows up into a holy temple in the Lord, in whom you too are built together into God's dwelling in the Spirit.

LORD Jesus Christ, our Cornerstone, look graciously on this work which we have commenced, and which we now dedicate to your glory (and to …). We ask you to bless ✠ this new edifice and grant continued safety to all who work here until that day when we can see this new enterprise begin to serve [*this parish, school, borough, whatever*] and give you glory; who live and reign for ever and ever. Amen.

TOPPING OFF A NEW BUILDING

PRAISE be to God, our Creator! We thank you, Lord, for the completion of this our enterprise, [grant us now the means to pay for it,] and we pray that its work may now tend to your glory and the salvation of humanity. Amen.

BLESSING OF A NEW MAYOR

LONGER FORM

The custom of each borough will clearly supply most of the form for this service, whereby the installation of a Mayor takes place in a Town Hall, or in the preferred church of the new Mayor. The following may, if wished, be taken simply as a resource to supplement the established procedure in each place.

In the name of the Father, and of the Son, ✠ and of the Holy Spirit. Amen.

℣. The Lord be with you.
℟. **And with your spirit.**

B ROTHERS and sisters, let us give thanks to God for the election of our new Mayor, Councillor N., and give thanks also for the work of his/her predecessor, Councillor N. We acknowledge God our heavenly Father as the source and inspiration of all earthly authority, and we pray his blessing upon the work of Mayor and Council for this coming year. In a moment of silence, let us make our prayers for them quietly, in our own way.

Silence is kept.

The following formulæ may be used where appropriate or desirable:

THE RED GOWN

R ECEIVE this gown, and remember the words of St Paul that charity should be our outward vesture. May its red colour remind you that your first duty is the defence of the rights of the citizens of this borough/city, for whom you should be prepared to shed your blood if necessary.

THE HAT

R ECEIVE this hat, and remember that you are the custodian, not the master, of the customs and traditions of this borough/city.

HEAVENLY Father, who commanded Moses to make vestments and regalia for those who ministered before your altars on behalf of your people, bless ✠, we pray, this chain of office which symbolizes the earthly authority and responsibility of the Mayor of N. Grant that he/she who wears it may remember well what it represents, and exercise his/her authority with honesty, responsibility and dignity, knowing that he/she will one day have to render account before you, the just judge on that day when all kingdoms, powers and sovereignties return to you their true owner, who live and reign for ever and ever. Amen.

The chain of office is placed on the new Mayor's shoulders.

RECEIVE this chain of office of the borough/city of N. Remember that just as the Son of Man came not be served, but to serve, so you, too, should be prepared to serve both God and your fellow citizens in this borough/city.

Councillors, Ladies and Gentlemen, I present to you your Mayor for this year of our Lord ...

Those present may indicate their approval by applause.

Other symbols of office may now be presented, such as keys to the Town Hall, or as is customary in the Borough, unless these be presented at another time.

The new Mayor kneels.

Let us pray.

ALMIGHTY God, fount and inspiration of all dignity and honour, of all that changes and all that endures, we pray that you bless ✠ with your heavenly grace N. our new Mayor. Endue him/her with your gifts of heavenly wisdom, and with prudence, courage, fortitude and patience. Make him/her unassuming in success, and generous in failure, rich in tact and fearless in leadership. Under his/her good government may this borough/city flourish for another year, and grow ever stronger in your grace. Through our Lord Jesus Christ your Son, who lives and reigns with you in the unity of the Holy Spirit, one God for ever and ever. Amen.

Shorter Installation of a Mayor

Let us pray.

ALMIGHTY God, we give thanks for the election of N. our new Mayor. We pray your blessing on him/her and this new council for this term of office. We pray for a spirit of charity and concord in all their deliberations, and a generous gift of wisdom and prudence. Together may they represent faithfully and well those whom they are elected to serve, and come with them to your kingdom, where you live and reign with Jesus Christ your Son and the Holy Spirit, one God for ever and ever. Amen.

May Almighty God bless this Mayor and Council: the Father, the Son ✠ and the Holy Spirit. Amen.

Council Meetings

A reading from the holy Gospel according to Mark.   10:42–45

JESUS said to the Apostles: You know that they who rule over the Gentiles lord it over them: and their princes have power over them. But it is not so among you: whosoever desires to be great must be your servant, and whosoever desires to be first among you shall be the servant of all. For the Son of man did not come to be served, but to serve, and to give his life as a redemption for many.

BRIEF PRAYER BEFORE COUNCIL MEETINGS

ALMIGHTY God, may our deliberations today be calm, charitable and fruitful. Guide our minds and our tongues to say what needs to be said concisely, eloquently and charitably. May our conclusions be prudent and our decisions be of genuine benefit to this borough/city. Amen.

A LONGER PRAYER

ALMIGHTY God, source of all authority and dignity, of stability and good government, we pray that you guide our minds with your inspiration and further all our doings with your powerful help. Incline us to the keeping of your laws and the promotion of good in all that we enact here today. May each one truly put the good of those whom they represent before all party distinction or competition, and before their own self-advancement or reputation. May our remarks be relevant, charitable and constructive and our decisions fruitful, that this borough/city may truly be a harmonious and happy witness to your goodness. Amen.

A SERVICE FOR THE BLESSING OF PETS

⚜

Let us pray.

HEAVENLY Father, glorious Creator of all that is good, who hate nothing that you have made, we gather to give you thanks today for the wonders of your creation, and especially for the goodness you show to us through these your creatures consigned to our care. Hear our prayer that we may be always attentive and responsible carers, and worthy dispensers of the care you show for us all. Through Christ our Lord. Amen.

A reading from the book of Genesis. 1:20–2:2

GOD said: let the waters bring forth multitudes of living creatures, and the birds that they may fly over the earth under the firmament of heaven. And God created the great whales, and every living and moving creature, which the waters brought forth, according to their kinds, and every winged fowl according to its kind. And God saw that it was good.

And he blessed them, saying: Increase and multiply, and fill the waters of the sea: and let the birds be multiplied upon the earth.

And the evening and the morning brought the fifth day.

And God said: Let the earth bring forth living creatures in their kind, cattle and creeping things, and beasts of the earth, according to their kinds. And so it was done.

And God made the beasts of the earth according to their kinds, and cattle, and every thing that creeps on the earth according to its kind. And God saw that it was good.

And he said: Let us make man in our image and likeness: and let him have dominion over the fishes of the sea, and the fowls of the air, and the beasts, and the whole earth, and every creeping creature that moves upon the earth.

And God created man in his own image: in the image of God he created him: male and female he created them.

And God blessed them, saying: Increase and multiply, and fill the earth, and subdue it, and rule over the fishes of the sea, and the fowls of the air, and all living creatures that move upon the earth.

And God said: Behold I have given you every plant bearing seed upon the earth, and all trees that have in themselves seed of their own kind, to be your food: and to all beasts of the earth, and to every fowl of the air, and to all that move upon the earth, everything that has life, that they may have food to feed upon. And so it was done.

And God saw all the things that he had made, and they were very good. And the evening and morning brought the sixth day.

So the heavens and the earth were finished, and all that filled them. And on the seventh day God ended his work which he had made: and he rested on the seventh day from all his work which he had done.

Let us pray.

HEAVENLY Father, good Creator, we ask you to bless ✠ these pets whom we love. As you created them in your abundant goodness for our comfort and companionship, we ask you to keep them healthy and happy. Make us careful tenders of your creation, being always aware of these creatures' needs that they may find joy in us as we do in them. Through our care of these pets may we become more able to care for our brothers and sisters and work for the furtherance of your Kingdom, where you live and reign for ever and ever. Amen.

Individual blessings may follow if thought desirable.

PART V

THROUGH THE YEAR

Seasonal prayers, blessings and other services

ADVENT

AN ADVENT WREATH

The advent wreath, originally a Norse pagan tradition, is a recent importation to the English-speaking world. It can be seen in its native element in Southern Germany and Austria, where instead of being a small tinsel-covered object, it takes the form of a cartwheel-sized, greenery-covered wheel suspended over the entrance to the sanctuary. There are only four candles and all are white. More commonly, advent wreaths are domestic; traditionally each new candle is lit after a reading of the Gospel for that Sunday. If the candles are to be lit at Mass, it clearly would not be a good idea to anticipate the Gospel, unless the lighting were to take place after the Gospel during Mass.

BLESSING

LORD Jesus Christ, the light of the world, we ask you to bless ✠ this Advent wreath, symbol of light in darkness. May we, who await your coming, be like the faithful virgins, ready at all times with lamps lit, that we may enter with you to the banquet of eternal life. Amen.

AT THE LIGHTING OF THE CANDLES

MAY the light of Christ rise in our hearts to dispel all darkness, and may his coming fill us with joy.

THE RORATE MASS

The Rorate Mass, or Missa Aurea, *is a common devotion for Advent especially in Southern Germany and Austria, and increasingly more widely. The tradition is that there should be a votive Mass of our Lady celebrated before the dawn by candlelight, and usually with music and white vestments. The name 'Rorate' is taken from the Introit antiphon in the Extraordinary Form for the third, Ember, Wednesday in Advent, traditionally the occasion for this Mass. These days the Rorate Mass is commonly celebrated on any free weekday in Advent. In the Extraordinary Form, the texts of the third Wednesday are used. In the Ordinary Form, the Mass from the Common of the Blessed Virgin Mary in Advent (Roman Missal p. 1107) may be used.*

CHRISTMASTIDE

THE CHRISTMAS MARTYROLOGY

The Martyrology is a sort of elaborate calendar, where day by day is written the list of the many saints whose feast day is celebrated on that day. The Christmas martyrology records also the birth of our Lord in a very striking way. It can be used in a number of ways, but is best sung (to the Old Testament Reading tone from the Graduale*) before Midnight Mass in a darkened church. It is customary to raise the tone when the cantor sings the passage 'Jesus Christ, eternal God … Virgin Mary'. If desired, the image of the Christ Child could be unveiled at this point. At the end of the Martyrology, the lights can be turned on, and Mass begins.*

First clause,   at the mid-point,   at the full stop

TRADITIONAL MARTYROLOGY TEXT

FIVE thousand, one hundred and ninety-nine years after the creation of the world, that time when God in the beginning made the heavens and the earth; two thousand nine hundred and fifty-seven years from the flood; two thousand and fifteen years after the birth of Abraham; one thousand five hundred and ten years from Moses, and the exodus of the children of Israel from Egypt; one thousand and thirty-two years from the anointing of King David; the sixty-fifth week according to the prophecy of Daniel; in the one hundred and ninety-fourth Olympiad; the seven hundred and fifty-second year since the foundation of the city of Rome; the forty-second year of the reign of Octavian Augustus, the whole earth being then at peace, Jesus Christ, eternal God, and the Son of the Eternal Father, wishing to make holy the world by his most merciful coming, having been conceived by the Holy Spirit, nine months from his conception was born in Bethlehem of Judea, made man of the Virgin Mary. The nativity of our Lord Jesus Christ according to the flesh.

COUNTLESS ages after the creation of the world when in the beginning God created the heavens and the earth and formed mankind in his image; and exceedingly long ages after the Most High set his bow in the clouds over the waters of the flood to be a sign of his covenant and of peace; twenty-one centuries from the migration of Abraham our father in faith from Ur of the Chaldees; thirteen centuries from the going forth of the people of Israel from Egypt at the leading of Moses; about a thousand years from the anointing of David as king; the sixty-fifth week according to the prophecy of Daniel; the one hundred and ninety-fourth Olympiad; the seven hundred and fifty-second year since the foundation of the city of Rome; in the forty-second year of the reign of Cæsar Octavian Augustus; all the earth being then at peace, Jesus Christ, everlasting God and Son of the eternal Father, devoutly wishing to consecrate the world by his coming, was conceived by the Holy Spirit and after the passage of nine months since his conception in Bethlehem of Judah was made man of the Virgin Mary: the nativity of our Lord Jesus Christ according to the flesh.

Private Blessing of a Small Crib

IN memory of the most holy incarnation of our Saviour, and to the honour of the most Holy Family, may this crib and all who pray before it be blessed in the name of the Father, and of the Son, ✠ and of the Holy Spirit. Amen.

BLESSING OF A CHRISTMAS CRIB
IN THE CONTEXT OF MIDNIGHT MASS

There are many ways of doing this. In many places, the Infant is carried in the entrance procession by either the celebrant or a small girl; the procession goes to the High Altar by way of the crib. There, the Infant is placed in the manger either before or after the blessing.

An alternative method is to have the Infant on the Sanctuary during Mass. In some places the image is unveiled at the point in the Gospel (or the Martyrology—see above) which tells of our Lord's birth. Then after Communion, the Infant is transferred to the crib.

HAIL and blessed be this hour and moment in which the Son of God was born of the most pure Virgin Mary at midnight in Bethlehem, in piercing cold. In this hour vouchsafe, O God, to hear our prayer and grant our desires, that those who come to pray before this image of your most holy incarnation may be granted all they need for body and soul, through the merits of our Saviour, Jesus Christ and of his blessed Mother. May this crib and all who pray here be blessed, in the name of the Father, and of the Son, ✠ and of the Holy Spirit. Amen.

Holy water. (Incense.) All may kneel.

DEVOUTLY we approach your cradle, Lord, to find the one of whom the prophets spoke, and here behold the mighty God of thunders lying helpless on the straw. O grant us some of this humility that we may conquer mightily the reign of sin within us. And grant us, too, the protection of your gentle mother, whose tender eye and loving heart attend your every wish. Who live and reign with your Father and the Holy Spirit, one God for ever and ever. Amen.

Prayer with the Audience before a Childrens' Nativity Play

L ORD God, who willed that your only Son be made flesh and dwell among us, we pray that as we remember his birth at Bethelehem we may renew our faith and wonder at this most glorious gift. And as your Son reminded us, since even the mouths of babes and sucklings may utter wisdom, may we take to heart those familiar mysteries we are about to see retold before us by our own children, and learn from those whom we teach. Through the same Christ our Lord. Amen.

Children's Gifts for the Poor

A little research can be done, perhaps with the assistance of the local social services, to find an institution or organization that cares for deprived children in this country or abroad. Shortly before Christmas, it is a good idea to encourage children to donate some toy (naturally in good condition) to benefit a child less well off.

L ORD Jesus Christ, who told us that it is more blessed to give than to receive, we thank you for all your goodness to us, and for all that we have been given by you and by our families. In particular we thank you for these gifts which you have given to us for a while, and which we are now happy to give to someone else to make their Christmas more joyful. We pray for the children who will receive these gifts; watch over them, Lord, and grant them good and loving families, with everything they need, especially this Christmastime. And make us always grateful for all the good things you have given us, who live and reign for ever and ever. Amen.

Grace before a Christmas Meal

Our Father.

℣. The Word was made flesh.
℞. **And dwelt amongst us.**

Let us pray.

L ORD God, who have given us all things in abundance, and did not even deny us your only Son to take flesh and to be born of the Virgin Mary for our salvation, we thank you once more for your kindness towards us, and we ask you to bless ✠ this food and those who prepared it. Keep this house in your care, and bless us your family who share this meal to honour your Son's holy nativity. Through the same Christ our Lord. Amen.

Blessing of Wine
on December 27, Feast of St John

According to tradition, St John the Evangelist was given a cup of poisoned wine which failed to harm him after he blessed it. This ancient blessing is taken from the Roman Ritual.

℣. Our help is in the name of the Lord.
℞. **Who made heaven and earth.**
℣. The Lord be with you.
℞. **And with your spirit.**

Let us pray.

B LESS ✠ and sanctify, Lord God, this cup of wine, and by the merits of St John the Evangelist, grant blessing and protection to all who believe and partake of this cup. And as St John was unharmed by the cup of poisoned wine, so may all who taste of this cup in his honour be protected against poison or any other harm, and making an offering of their souls and bodies, may they be freed from all sin. Through Christ our Lord. Amen.

BLESS this cup, O Lord, that it may be a remedy for all who taste of it, and grant that by the invocation of your holy name all who drink from it may receive from you health in mind and body. Through Christ our Lord. Amen.

And may the blessing of Almighty God, Father, Son ✠ and Holy Spirit, descend on this wine and on whoever tastes it, and remain for ever. Amen.

Holy water.

NEW YEAR SERVICE

This is another season of the year where there is no particular liturgy associated with it, other than the normal public worship of the Church, which celebrates the Feast of Mary, Mother of God. However, in peoples' minds it is a significant day in its own right, and hence worth addressing religiously.

There are many possibilities. One which the Methodists use is the Covenant Renewal service, which can be found in another context in this book on p. 165. Other places observe a period of exposition of the Blessed Sacrament leading up to Benediction at the stroke of midnight. It would seem appropriate to review the main events of the passing year and commend them to God, and likewise pray for the anticipated events of the coming year. People can be encouraged to make their New Year's resolutions before God, which gives them a little more motivation for keeping to them.

A FAMILY BLESSING
ON THE FEAST OF THE HOLY FAMILY

LORD God, who blessed the human family when you willed that your only-begotten Son should live under the protection of St Joseph and the Blessed Virgin Mary, we ask your blessing ✠ on this family/these families/the families of our parish. May their love for each other reflect your own love for us; keep them safe together through the storms of life, and may they all come safely one day to heaven, where you live and reign for ever and ever. Amen.

The Epiphany

Proclamation of the Year of Salvation

After the Gospel at the principal Mass in the cathedral church (and if desired, also in parish churches), the following proclamation of the year of Salvation should be made solemnly (and preferably sung, to the Exsultet tone) from the ambo. The current edition of the Roman Missal, p. 1505, includes a different translation of this with music.

BROTHERS and sisters: we have already rejoiced at the celebration of our Lord's birth. Now it is our happiness to proclaim to you the day when we will celebrate his resurrection, and the days for those feasts of the Church which depend upon it.

On the N.th day of N. the holy fast of Lent will begin with the penitential day of Ash Wednesday. And so the holy Passover of the Lord and his glorious resurrection from the dead will be celebrated on Easter Sunday: the N.th day of N. The holy feast of the Ascension of our Lord Jesus Christ will be celebrated on the N.th day of N., and on the N.th day of N. falls the Solemnity of Pentecost. The holy festival of the Body and Blood of Christ will be celebrated on the N.th day of N., and the N.th day of N. will be the first Sunday of Advent as we await the coming of our Lord Jesus Christ, to whom be glory and honour for ever and ever. Amen.

Blessing of Gold, Incense and Myrrh

Gifts of money for the Church, incense, and alms for the poor may be presented for use in the Church for worship throughout the year. These, or a representative portion, may be taken to the crib and presented there.

℣. Our help is in the name of the Lord.
℟. **Who made heaven and earth.**

℣. The Lord be with you.
℟. **And with your spirit.**

Let us pray.

RECEIVE, O Lord, from us, your unworthy servants, these gifts which we present in honour of your holy name and in acknowledgement of your great power. Accept them as you accepted the gift of righteous Abel, and as you accepted these same gifts from the magi who came from afar. Lord Jesus Christ, fill them with your heavenly blessing as we consecrate them to your worship, acknowledging your kingship and divinity and honouring your painful death and glorious resurrection.

So may the blessing of Almighty God, Father, Son ✠ and Holy Spirit, sanctify these gifts in honour of his holy Epiphany.

Epiphany Home Blessings

This blessing is most commonly carried out in Southern Germany and Austria, where all homes in the parish are systematically blessed during the Epiphany season. As a sign of the blessing, the doorposts are marked with chalk.

The Blessing of Chalk

℣. Our help is in the name of the Lord.
℟. **Who made heaven and earth.**
℣. The Lord be with you.
℟. **And with your spirit.**

Let us pray.

BLESS, ✠ O Lord, this chalk and grant salvation to the human race. May all who cause the names of your holy magi Caspar, Melchior and Balthasar to be inscribed above their doors be blessed by the invocation of your most holy name, enjoy health of mind and body, and experience your strong protection for their souls. Through Christ our Lord. Amen.

AT THE HOMES:

℣. Peace be to this place.
℟. **And to all who dwell here.**

Antiphon. From the east came magi to Bethlehem to adore the Lord; and opening their treasures they offered precious gifts: gold for the great king, frankincense for the true God, and myrrh for his entombment, alleluia.

As the Magnificat is recited, the interior of the house is sprinkled with holy water.

M y soul ✠ magnifies the Lord,
   my spirit rejoices in God who is my Saviour,
who has looked upon the humility of his handmaiden.
Behold, all generations from now will acknowledge me blessed,
For the mighty one has done great things for me:
   Holy is his name!
His mercy is from one generation to the next on those who fear him.
   Mighty is his arm!
He has scattered the proud in the imagination of their hearts,
   and has put down the powerful from their thrones,
   exalting those of humble degree.
The hungry he has filled with good things,
   but the rich he has dismissed with nothing.
Remembering his mercy, he has helped his servant Israel,
   as he promised to our fathers,
   to Abraham and to his posterity for evermore.
Glory be ...

Ant. From the east came magi to Bethlehem to adore the Lord; and opening their treasures they offered precious gifts: gold for the great king, frankincense for the true God, and myrrh for his entombment, alleluia.

Our Father.
℣. O Lord, hear my prayer,
℟. **And let my cry come to you.**
℣. The Lord be with you.
℟. **And with your spirit.**

Let us pray.

O GOD, who, by the leading of a star revealed your only-begotten Son to the nations, grant in your mercy that we who now know you by faith may one day be led to the contemplation of your heavenly splendour. Through the same Christ our Lord. Amen.

℣. Arise, Jerusalem, shine out, for your light has come, and the glory of the Lord has risen upon you:
℟. **He is Christ the Lord, born of the Virgin Mary.**

℣. And the nations shall walk in your light, and kings in the splendour of your rising.
℟. **He is Christ the Lord, born of the Virgin Mary.**

L ORD God Almighty, we ask you to bless ✠ this place, that herein may be found health, purity, triumphant virtue, humility, goodness, tolerance, law-abidingness, and thanksgiving to God the Father, Son and Holy Spirit; and may their blessing remain for ever upon this place and all who dwell (or work) here. Through Christ our Lord. Amen.

In many places it is customary to use the blessed chalk to mark on the outside of the principal door's lintel the numerals of the current year separated by crosses and the initial letters of the three magi:

20 C+M+B 18

CANDLEMAS

FEBRUARY 2

This feast commemorates the presentation of our Lord in the temple and also the ritual purification of the Blessed Virgin Mary. Now that the feast of the Circumcision is no longer celebrated, this feast has subsumed to some extent the theme of our Lord's willing subjection to the Law of Moses.

It would be a shame to skimp the ceremonies of this day; they are very eloquent and beautiful, appealing particularly to children. The compiler has used the candle service and procession (without Mass) very successfully in primary schools.

For the parish, this feast is a good opportunity to buy (or invite people to buy for the parish) the year's stocks of candles and to bless them. It was a pre-Reformation English custom to bless the Paschal Candle with the others, and to have it carried (unlit) in the procession. There is no reason why people may not bring their own candles to be blessed on this day, or candles may be offered (sold?) to the people to take home with them. At any rate, it is preferable to present candles which are rather more substantial than the votive lights used in some places.

All texts can be found in the Missal.

THE FEAST OF ST BLAISE
February 3

The Blessing of Throats

Two candles of at least 8 inches' length are bound together crosswise, fastened with ribbon. These should be left with holy water on a table in the sanctuary. After Mass, the candles may be blessed as follows:

O GOD, almighty and yet gentle, who created all things by your only Word, and brought about the recreation of humanity by the means of that same Word by whom all things were made, and who became flesh for our sakes, who are mighty and immense, terrible and worthy of all praise, worker of wonders, for whose confession of faith the glorious bishop and martyr Blaise did not tremble before the multitude of his torments, and bravely won the palm of martyrdom; the same God who mercifully granted, among so many other gifts, healing of the throat: we pray that despite our unworthiness, and by the merits of the same Saint Blaise you might bless ✠ these candles and through them infuse your grace, that the throats of all they touch may be healed of every affliction of the throat, returning to the church healthy and happy, there to raise their voices to the praise of your holy name, which is blessed for evermore. Through our Lord Jesus Christ your Son, who lives and reigns with you in the unity of the Holy Spirit, one God for ever and ever. Amen.

The candles are sprinkled with holy water. Each throat is then blessed by holding the candles scissor-wise (unlit!) around the throat of each person, saying:

BY the intercession of Saint Blaise, Bishop and Martyr, may God free you from illness of the throat and from all other evils. In the name of the Father, and of the Son, ✠ and of the Holy Spirit. Amen.

Blessing of Food
against illness of the throat, on St Blaise's Day

In the blessing, taken from the Roman Ritual, the foods specified are bread, wine, water and fruit.

℣. Our help is in the name of the Lord.
℟. Who made heaven and earth.
℣. The Lord be with you.
℟. And with your spirit.

Let us pray.

LORD God, Saviour of the world, who have consecrated this day to the honour of St Blaise the martyr, to whom among other graces you gave the power to cure illness of the throat: we pray your infinite mercy that you bless ✠ and sanctify this bread, wine, water and fruit which your people have brought, that whoever tastes of them may be freed from sickness of the throat and all other infirmity of body or soul by the merits and intercession of the same St Blaise, your bishop and martyr; who live and reign for ever and ever. Amen.

LENT

A PARISH PROJECT

To have some specific charitable project for which funds will be gathered through Lent is a good way to unite a parish. It can also be pastorally useful to insist that nobody simply dips into their pockets for this project, but that every penny must be raised by some means. In this way, one discovers new talents in the parish, parishioners meet one another and make friends, and the benefits go far beyond simple moneymaking.

A LENTEN RULE

Having something written down is always useful, and something along these lines could be duplicated and left in the church for people to pick up and use.

LENT; WHAT IS IT ABOUT?

OUR souls, like our bodies, get run down. Lent is a time for spiritual training; for raising ideals, for practising exercises and virtues in the hope that they may have permanent effect, and for doing penance for our sins.

But we must be practical, not vague. It is better to choose one penance and stick to it, rather than aiming to do too much and failing in fact to do anything. Use this card to write down what you want to achieve, keep it by you, and assess how you have done each night.

FOUR THINGS TO AIM FOR DURING LENT 20…

• Acquiring a particular virtue is in many ways more practical than trying to wipe out a particular sin. For instance, if tempted to gossip or scandal, try finding each day specific kind things to say about people. If the temptations are to envy or jealousy, try being especially kind to the person of whom one is envious; if to sloth, specific energetic acts can be undertaken. Then there is that long put-off fitness plan …

• The practice of a particular devotion is also an important part of Lent. For instance, you might consider coming to Mass during the week, or saying the rosary: any particular undertaking is a good idea, as is regular prayer for a particular intention.

• A particular penance is the most traditional form of Lenten observance, and is vital for training the will. If we cannot even control our appetite for a cigarette, or a spoon of sugar in our tea, how can we hope to control a harsh temper or a cruel tongue?

• Almsgiving is also vitally important. We remember that there are so many people in the world worse off than ourselves, and we set aside part of our income, or take the trouble to earn money for those less fortunate.

It is wise every day to pray for strength to fulfil your intentions, and each evening to consider how your resolutions have held up during the day.

My resolutions for Lent 20...

The VIRTUE at which I will aim is ...

The DEVOTION that I will undertake is ...

The PENANCE that I will do is ...

I will give ALMS to ...

       (Signed)......................................

       (Date)..

The Quarant'ore
the forty hours' devotion

The Forty Hours' Devotion, or Quarant' Ore, is a period of extended exposition of the Blessed Sacrament, possibly originally taken from the forty hours or so that our Lord's body rested in the tomb. The practice grew up in sixteenth-century Italy, and became officially recognized and encouraged in 1592 with Pope Clement VIII's constitution Graves et Diuturnæ *which urged all Christians to take on the Forty Hours' Devotion, praying especially for peace. It can be celebrated at any time of the year, but Lent particularly suggests itself.*

It is customary to expose the Blessed Sacrament with particular splendour, though it is not considered necessary these days to expose for forty continuous hours; this may be impractical in certain places, but the period should certainly be extended. At no time should be Blessed Sacrament be left without somebody in Church watching and praying; to this end, lists should be prepared where people may sign their names and undertake to watch for periods of half an hour or so. Naturally in this work clergy and extraordinary ministers of the Eucharist should take a lead.

Formerly it was customary to celebrate Masses before the Blessed Sacrament exposed (or sometimes hidden with a screen). This is now forbidden, and so the Blessed Sacrament should be reposed in the tabernacle before each Mass during the period of exposition; small Masses could perhaps take place at a side altar out of sight of the altar of exposition.

If it is decided not to extend the watching during the night, when the Blessed Sacrament is reposed, it may be done either without ceremony or with Benediction.

PREPARATIONS

2 weeks before:

> Watching lists put out at the back of the Church for people to volunteer.
> Extra candles ordered.
> Neighbouring parishes encouraged to advertise and participate.

Immediate preparation:

> Any images around the altar of exposition should be removed or covered.

THE FIRST DAY: MASS OF EXPOSITION.

This is a votive Mass of the Blessed Sacrament, with white vestments. It is preferable that the Host for exposition be consecrated at this Mass; in this case, it remains on the altar during the distribution of Communion. This being done, the celebrant, at the altar, reads the Postcommunion prayer, and then exposes the Blessed Sacrament in the usual way. A Eucharistic hymn may be sung (such as O Salutaris Hostia*) and the Blessed Sacrament censed and enthroned.*

It is traditional at this juncture to have a procession of the Blessed Sacrament in the church (it is not necessary to go outside). If it is decided to do this, all should proceed as on Maundy Thursday; after the postcommunion prayer the celebrant may remove his chasuble and change into a cope. The Blessed Sacrament is exposed on the altar. Incense is placed in two thuribles, and the procession moves off with all taking part carrying candles. It is traditional for the Blessed Sacrament to be covered with a canopy during the procession, and eucharistic hymns may be sung. It is customary that the last hymn be Pange Lingua *('Of the Glorious Body telling'), pausing if necessary before the last two verses. On return to the sanctuary the Blessed Sacrament is enthroned, the last two verses of* Pange Lingua (Tantum ergo *and* Genitori genitoque*) are sung, and the Blessed Sacrament censed. At this point it is customary to sing or recite the whole Great Litany (see p. 153). Benediction may (but need not) be given. The servers and clergy genuflect and withdraw.*

THE SECOND DAY

Some time during this day a solemn votive Mass for peace may be celebrated. The Blessed Sacrament should be reposed in the tabernacle without fuss or ceremony before the Mass, and exposed and enthroned likewise again after. It is forbidden to celebrate Mass before the Blessed Sacrament exposed.

THE THIRD DAY

It is traditional to have a Solemn Mass of Deposition ending with another procession and Benediction. However, since it might be thought strange to depose the Blessed Sacrament for the Mass, then expose it again momentarily only to carry it round the church and repose it again, some thought needs to be given as to how to manage this. Some places omit the Mass altogether, having instead a splendid closing Benediction. It could be combined with a procession, as on the first day, ending with the Benediction. This seems to be the best solution.

LÆTARE (MOTHERING) SUNDAY

There are no particular ceremonies or prayers associated with this day other than those of the liturgy, which reflects a conscious lightening of the Lenten discipline. Even the vestments may be of rose pink colour. Nonetheless, since mothers are unquestionably in most people's minds on this day, it would seem good to reflect on this in some way; perhaps by an act of devotion in honour of the Mother of God. The following prayer may be used.

A PRAYER FOR MOTHERS

A LMIGHTY God, who willed that your only-begotten Son be born of a woman, we pray now for the mothers you have given us, whether they are alive or have died. We thank you for the lessons we have learnt from them, for the love and sacrifice that they have made for us; these things have taught us something of your own eternal love, and so we pray that you enfold our mothers in that same love, wherever they may be, and bring them one day to heaven, where you live and reign with your Son in the unity of the Holy Spirit, one God for ever and ever. Amen.

BLESSING OF FLOWERS

L ORD God, who willed that your Son should be born of a woman, and so share with us the joy and privilege of having a mother to love and be loved by, bless ✠, we pray, these flowers dedicated to the honour of our heavenly mother, and to the joy of our earthly mothers. May they be a sign of our love, gratitude and appreciation of all that we have received from them. Through Christ our Lord. Amen.

PASSIONTIDE

VEILING OF STATUES

It is customary that during the last two weeks of Lent all images, including crucifixes, be either covered or removed, the better to focus upon the coming commemoration of the Lord's passion. It would seem better to veil, rather than remove, the images, as the effect is more striking that way. There is no ceremony involved in this, though some care might be given to arranging the purple veiling in such a way that it can be quickly and easily removed during the Gloria at the Easter Vigil, which is more eloquent than doing so beforehand.

TENEBRÆ

The Church recommends that during the Easter Triduum (Maundy Thursday, Good Friday, Holy Saturday) the Office of Readings and Lauds ('Morning Prayer') be celebrated together with the people. This recalls the service known as Tenebræ, commonly celebrated in larger churches in former years, in which the offices of Matins and Lauds were combined, featuring some of the most affecting music of the Church's year: the Lamentations of Jeremiah, the various settings of the Tenebræ Responsories and the Miserere by Allegri all formed part of this dramatic service in which a large fifteen-branch candlestick (the 'hearse') formed the focus, one candle being extinguished at the conclusion of each psalm.

Adapting the traditional ceremonies of Tenebræ to the new rite should pose no particular difficulty. Some thought may be given as to the best time to celebrate it; until the Holy Week reforms of the 1950s, the service took place on the evening before (thus, Maundy Thursday Tenebræ, 'darkness', was celebrated on Wednesday night, and so forth). Unquestionably the darkness made for a more impressive service, but the Church does not encourage us to anticipate Lauds these days.

The Office of Readings and Lauds each have three psalms, making six psalms or canticles in total. An ordinary Benediction seven-branch candlestick is ideal for use as a 'hearse'. It should be placed on a stand in the sanctuary (traditionally somewhat to the right hand side, set at an angle), and the candles (unbleached if possible) all lit before the service begins. The altar candles should also be lit on Maundy Thursday and Holy

Saturday. As the service proceeds, a server should snuff one candle on the seven-branch candlestick at the end of each psalm (not, however, the Invitatory psalm, which can, of course, be omitted). During the Benedictus, the altar candles are snuffed and the lights in the church gradually turned off. There should be one candle remaining burning on the seven-branch candlestick (traditionally the one in the middle), which the server removes and places behind the altar, so that it cannot be seen (a candlestick placed there before the service would be a good idea). The Celebrant reads the collect, and when it has concluded, strikes his book hard against his seat; all present do the same. After a few seconds of noise, the server brings the lit candle from behind the altar and places it on the altar itself. This is all to symbolize the death of our Lord, the chaos attendant on it, and how the resurrection restores order to the world. The office is concluded, and all withdraw in silence.

Maundy Thursday

The Agape

The washing of feet at the Mass of the Lord's Supper is optional; this is an alternative way of fulfilling the Lord's Mandatum, or command, derived from the practice outlined in the Sarum Missal. The suggestion is that this should take place near the church, before the Mass of the Lord's Supper.

Remote preparation: a sign-up list for people to signal their attendance and state what their food contribution will be. The food should be simple and, given the season, preferably vegetarian. Someone should bake a loaf of unleavened bread.

On the day: lay a table for all, with cloths and other decorations. Several jugs of warm water, bowls, and towels. A loving cup should be made up; the contents can be anything pleasant to drink: various recipes can be found on the internet. The unleavened loaf should be placed prominently. A Bible should be prepared, or at least the text of St John's Gospel.

First Part: the Mandatum

John 13:1–15 is read.

The priest or leader then washes some feet, and then all participants must wash at least one other person's foot or feet.

Meanwhile, the following psalms are recited with their antiphons before and after.

1) *Antiphon:* I give you a new commandment: love one another as I have loved you, says the Lord.

   Psalm 67(66) (O God, be gracious and bless us)

2) *Ant.* Let us love one another, for love is from God, and whoever loves brother and sister is a child of God and will see God.

   Psalm 133(132) (How good and how pleasant it is)

3) *Ant.* Mary washed the feet of Jesus, and dried them with her hair, and the whole house was full of the scent of the ointment.

   Psalm 118 (119) vv. 1–16 (They are happy whose life is blameless)

When all feet have been washed, the following prayers are said:

℣. O God, we have received your mercy,
℟. **In the midst of your temple.**

℣. All your commands, O Lord,
℟. **You have directed that we should keep them.**

℣. Behold, how good and how joyful it is
℟. **When brethren live in harmony**

℣. O Lord, hear my prayer.
℟. **And let my cry come to you.**

℣. The Lord be with you.
℟. **And with your spirit.**

Let us pray.

COME to us, we pray O Lord Jesus, in our work; and as you washed the feet of your disciples, see that your servants have done the same thing and fulfilled your command. Grant that, as we have washed off the exterior dirt of our bodies, in the same way we may be be washed interiorly of our sins, who live and reign with the Father and the Holy Spirit, one God for ever and ever. Amen.

THIRD PART: THE AGAPE MEAL

Bread is now broken and shared, and a loving cup is passed around. Meanwhile, John 13:16–38 is read.

When this has been done, the meal is shared and then cleared away. When all have finished, the Gospel is continued: John 14:1–31. With the words Rise, let us go from here, *all rise and go to the church for the Mass of the Lord's Supper. There should be ample space between finishing the meal and Communion to fulfil the Eucharistic Fast.*

EASTER AND PASCHALTIDE

The Easter Blessing of Food
Święconka

It is an ancient custom still practised widely among Poles to bring a basket of food to the church to be blessed on Holy Saturday. Baskets are prepared containing butter (often formed into a lamb or cross), bread (often baked with the symbol of a cross or a fish), horseradish for the passion of Christ, eggs, sausage, ham, smoked bacon, salt and cheese. Most of these foods were traditionally not eaten during Lent. In the basket should also be a candle, and everything covered over with a linen cloth. The basket can be decorated with ribbons and greenery. The three blessings following are used, holy water being sprinkled each time. For this purpose, it will be necessary to reserve a little holy water.

Let us ask Christ our Lord, who is always present among those who love him, to bless these foods for the Easter table.

Everyone prays for a moment in silence.

LORD Jesus Christ, who the day before your Passion and Death, commanded your disciples to prepare the Passover supper; and who on the day of the Resurrection accepted the invitation of two disciples and sat down with them at table; and who in the late evening came to the Apostles to eat with them: we pray that in faith we may experience your presence among us during our festive meal on the day of your victory, so that we may rejoice in your life and resurrection.

THE BLESSING OF BREAD

LIVING Bread, who descended from heaven and who as Holy Communion give life to the world, bless ✠ this bread and all Easter bread as a remembrance of that bread with which you fed the people who followed you in the wilderness, and the bread which after your resurrection you prepared by the lakeside for your disciples.

LAMB of God, who conquered evil and cleansed the world of sins, bless ✠ this meat, ham, and all the food which we will eat as a remembrance of the Paschal Lamb and of the festive dishes which you ate with the Apostles at the Last Supper.

THE BLESSING OF SALT

Bless also ✠ our salt to protect us from corruption.

THE BLESSING OF EGGS

CHRIST, our life and our resurrection, bless ✠ these eggs, a sign of new life, so that we may share together in our families, together with relatives and guests, the joy that you are with us. May we all come to your eternal banquet where you live and reign for ever and ever. Amen.

The baskets are now sprinkled with holy water.

BLESSING OF HOMES IN PASCHALTIDE
SEE P. 45

MAY

MONTH OF OUR BLESSED LADY

❧ ✠ ❧

CROWNING OF OUR LADY'S STATUE
AND PROCESSION

May is a good time to remind people of the importance of devotion to our Lady. It is traditional for there to be a procession, carrying an image of our Lady in the place of honour, and singing Marian hymns. At some point, a young girl crowns the image with flowers. Alternatively, the crowning could take place in the context of the main Mass on the first Sunday of May.

It is also a good month to undertake a parish pilgrimage to one or another Marian shrine, and to encourage people to learn how to say the rosary.

MAY 3: FINDING OF THE HOLY CROSS

BLESSING OF RODS ('CROSSES') TO SUPPORT CLIMBING PLANTS

This blessing could easily be adapted to bless agricultural or gardening implements during the planting season.

℣. Our help is in the name of the Lord.
℟. Who made heaven and earth.
℣. The Lord be with you.
℟. And with your spirit.

Let us pray.

ALMIGHTY and eternal God, Father of all mercies and consolation: by the merits of the most bitter passion of your Son who was raised on the wood of the Cross on behalf of us sinners, bless ✠ these rods which your faithful people have brought to be placed in gardens, vineyards, fields and other places, that wherever they will be placed may be kept free from the damage of hail, the blast of the wind, the tumult of storms and every infestation of the enemy; may their fruits grow to ripeness, to be collected to your honour by those who place their hope in the power of the holy Cross of the same Lord Jesus Christ, who lives and reigns with you for ever and ever. Amen.

BEFORE THE ASCENSION

THE ROGATION PROCESSION

On Monday, Tuesday or Wednesday of Ascension week, there is the custom of walking in solemn procession through the fields, or around the bounds of the parish, or even around the church grounds singing or reciting the Great Litany: see p. 153.

CORPUS CHRISTI

THE CELEBRATION OF FIRST HOLY COMMUNIONS

It is customary on or around the solemnity of Corpus et Sanguis Christi *to give children their first Holy Communion, they having achieved the age of reason (and thus able to understand the distinction between ordinary and consecrated eucharistic bread), and having been instructed. There are no special rules for this ceremony; arrangements are entirely according to tradition and thus may be modified as seems good.*

It is almost universally customary for girls to dress as brides, and boys to dress smartly: school uniform is often used, sometimes with the addition of a coloured sash. It is a good idea for a parish where there may be economic hardship to keep a small stock of suitable girls' white dresses and veils so that none may feel left out.

In many parishes the children process in before the priest and take their places together at the front of the church. In this case it is wise that they be accompanied at all times by a responsible adult. In some places the children carry their baptismal candles which may be lit for the reception of communion. In this case, obviously, communion should be received on the tongue only. There are no particular ceremonies concerned with the reception of communion, other than that girls should remove any gloves if they are to receive on the hand. It is customary that the children receive before the rest of the congregation; in some places it is customary that the children be joined by the rest of their family to receive. This may pose problems logistically unless the children have been sitting with the rest of the family through the Mass.

After the Mass it is customary to serve the children a First Communion Breakfast. It is also customary that in parishes which celebrate an outdoor procession of the Blessed Sacrament on or around the same day, that the children who have just received their first Communion wear their Communion outfits and play a special role which will be described below.

THE OUTDOOR PROCESSION
OF THE BLESSED SACRAMENT

In temperate climates this is always a little risky, due to the weather. But it is worth doing, and makes a strong impression on the participants if it is done well.

PREPARE:

In the church, everything for Benediction of the Blessed Sacrament. Two thuribles, canopy (outside the sanctuary). Torches with wind protection (clear plastic drinking glasses with the bottom cut off do well). Outside, one or more altars where Benediction will be given en route, equipped with candles, flowers &c.

JUNE 23: EVE OF ST JOHN THE BAPTIST

⟨᭒⟩

BLESSING OF A BONFIRE

Bonfires on Midsummer night were a nearly-universal feature of European life until relatively recently. They are still lit this night in many places.

℣. Our help is in the name of the Lord.
℟. Who made heaven and earth.
℣. The Lord be with you.
℟. And with your spirit.

Let us pray.

L ORD God, almighty Father, undying light, Creator of all light: bless ✠ this new fire, we pray, and grant that after the darkness of this age we may be worthy with pure minds to approach you, the light that never dies. Through Christ our Lord. Amen.

The fire is blessed with holy water, and then the ancient hymn to St John the Baptist, Ut queant laxis, *is sung.*

D *o* let our voices *re*sonate most purely,
 *Mi*racles telling, *far* greater than many;
So let our tongues be *la*vish in thy praises,
    Saint John the Baptist.

Lo! a swift herald, from the skies descending,
Bears to thy father promise of thy greatness;
How he shall name thee, what thy future story,
    Duly revealing.

Scarcely believing message so transcendent,
Him for a season power of speech forsaketh,
Till, at thy wondrous birth, again returneth
    Voice to the voiceless.

Thou, in thy mother's womb all darkly cradled,
Knewest thy Monarch, biding in his chamber,
Whence the two parents, through their children's merits,
 Mysteries utter'd.

Unto the Father, and the Sole-Begotten,
And to the Spirit, one in might and splendour
Glory undying, let us praise for ever,
 Glorious Trinity. Amen.

First verse tr. Cecile Gertken OSB

℣. There was a man sent by God.
℟. His name was John.

Let us pray.

O GOD, who made this day great by the birth of Saint John, grant to your people the grace of spiritual joy, and direct the feet of your faithful people in the way of eternal salvation. Through Christ our Lord. Amen.

AUGUST 15: ASSUMPTION
OF THE BLESSED VIRGIN MARY

ളへ⁂ⴷ

BLESSING OF VEGETABLES AND FRUITS

This is an early harvest thanksgiving for the bounty of the summer. The text is a shorter version of the long blessing in the ancient Roman Ritual.

℣ The Lord has given his blessing.
℞. **And the earth has given its fruit.**

℣. You water the heights of the mountains.
℞. **The earth is refreshed with your rain.**

℣. Giving grass to feed the beasts,
℞. **And plants to serve man's needs.**

℣. That you might bring bread from the earth,
℞. **And wine to cheer men's hearts.**

℣. Oil to make their faces shine,
℞. **And bread to make them strong.**

℣. Our help is in the name of the Lord.
℞. **Who made heaven and earth.**

℣. The Lord be with you.
℞. **And with your spirit.**

Let us pray.

ALMIGHTY ever-living God, who by your word created out of nothing the heavens, the earth, the sea, things visible and invisible, and furnished the earth with plants and trees for the use of man and beast; who commanded each species to bring forth fruit in its kind, for the food of the living and the healing of the sick: with heart and lips we pray you in your great mercy to bless ✠ these vegetables and fruits, increasing their natural powers with the new grace of your blessing. May they be a strong protection against all sickness and adversity for the men and beasts who will use them in your name. Through Christ our Lord. Amen.

May the blessing of almighty God, Father, Son ✠ and Holy Spirit, descend upon this harvest and remain for ever. Amen.

HARVEST THANKSGIVING

꧁ ✤ ꧂

Psalm 66 (67) is very appropriate, and may be used at any of these services.

MAY God be gracious and bless us,
May he shine the light of his face upon us
And may he have mercy on us.

That we may know your ways upon earth,
Your saving power for all the nations.

Let the people praise you, O God,
Let all the people praise you!

Let the nations be glad and rejoice,
For you judge the people with justice,
You direct the nations on earth.

Let the people praise you, O God,
Let all the people praise you!

The earth has now given its fruit;
May God, our God now bless us.

Indeed may God now bless us
Till all the ends of the earth learn to love him.

HARVEST BLESSING IN A SCHOOL

A reading from the book of Genesis.   1:10–12

GOD called the dry land 'Earth', and the water gathered together he called
'Sea', and God saw that it was good. God said 'Let the earth bring forth green
plants to produce seeds, and trees to bear fruit of every kind which will also
contain seeds.' And so it was done. The earth brought forth green plants and
the trees bore fruit of every kind with seeds in it, and God saw that it was good.

and/or

A reading from the book of Leviticus.   19:9–10

THE Lord spoke to Moses, saying: 'When you reap the corn on your land,
do not cut down all that is on your land completely, or collect all the grain

that falls on the ground. Nor should you pick up the bunches and grapes that fall to the ground in your vineyard, but leave them for the poor and the strangers to eat. I am the Lord your God.'

Let us pray.

HEAVENLY Father, we thank you for all the good things our earth has produced, as you commanded. You have provided for us yet again, and given us more food and drink that we need. Now we are glad to return some of that so that others who do not have enough may benefit from your kindness. Help us always to remember, when we are full, that others are empty. Help us to create good habits of generosity in ourselves because you, Father, have been generous to us. Finally, we ask you bless these gifts we have given for those who need them, in the name of the Father, and of the Son, ✠ and of the Holy Spirit. Amen.

HARVEST BLESSING IN CHURCH

The Roman Missal *and* Common Worship *both contain Eucharistic celebrations for the Harvest. This blessing is for use outside the Mass, or in the context of another celebration.*

A reading from the book of Leviticus. 23:9–11

THE Lord spoke to Moses, saying "Speak to the children of Israel, and say to them: 'When you have entered the land which I will give you, and have reaped your corn, you must bring sheaves, the firstfruits of your harvest to the priest. He must lift up the sheaves before the Lord on the day after the Sabbath, so that they may be acceptable for you, and he shall bless them.

Let us pray.

ALMIGHTY God, bless ✠ these gifts which we have laid before you, symbols of all that you have created and have given to humanity to strengthen the body and cheer the soul. As a sign of our gratitude, we dedicate these symbols of your bounty to the benefit of those who are in need, that they, too, may rejoice in your goodness. Through Christ our Lord. Amen.

Grace Before a Harvest Supper

FATHER of all goodness, who have provided from your store such bounty for all men and beasts, we ask you to bless ✠ us and this meal which we share in thanksgiving for this year's harvest. Bless, too, all those who have laboured to produce this food on our farms and in our factories, and those who have worked so hard today to prepare this meal for us to enjoy. As we taste the first fruits of your goodness, we remember your command not to forget those who lack the abundance we celebrate today, and we ask your blessing on them for better times and healthy harvests. Now, dear Lord, grant us healthy appetites, good cheer and great thankfulness for food, drink and fellowship. Amen.

NOVEMBER
MONTH OF THE HOLY SOULS

Annual Blessing of a Cemetery

This is most commonly celebrated on the first Sunday after All Souls' Day. If it is possible to begin in a church or other building, the paschal candle may be placed, lit, in the sanctuary. Holy water should be prepared, as well as candles in wind-protecting containers for the faithful to place on graves later. If it is necessary to hold the entire service in the open air, common-sense adaptations should be made. All may begin with a suitable hymn.

In the name of the Father, and of the Son, ✠ and of the Holy Spirit. Amen.

℣. The Lord be with you.
℟. And with your spirit.

Let us pray.

ALMIGHTY God, who by the three days' resting of your only Son in the tomb sanctified the graves of all who die in the hope of resurrection: grant peace and eternal light to those whom we love, buried in this cemetery or elsewhere, and strengthen our faith that both we and they will together rise again, as Jesus did on the third day, to behold you, our only true and eternal God, in our flesh. Through the same Jesus Christ our Lord, who lives and reigns with you and the Holy Spirit, one God for ever and ever. Amen.

A suitable piece of scripture may be read at this point; for example, from the Lectionary's selection of texts for funerals. This could be followed by a brief homily.

INTERCESSIONS

JESUS, who promised joy to those who mourn, and himself wept at the death of Lazarus, is close to us as we pray for the souls of those who have died. Let us confidently ask him to bring those who have died speedily to heaven and comfort the sorrowful.

Lord, grant rest to those who have died violently.
℣. Lord, in your mercy,
℟. hear our prayer.

Grant rest to those who have died young, or in tragic circumstances.
℣. Lord, in your mercy …

Grant rest to those who have no-one to pray for them.
℣. Lord, in your mercy …

Grant rest to those we love who have died, and whose names we now call to mind.
(long pause)
℣. Lord, in your mercy …

And grant comfort to ourselves and to all who mourn.
℣. Lord, in your mercy …

May Mary, kindest comforter of the afflicted, and mother of all Holy Souls, intercede for all her children as we say: Hail Mary.

HEAVENLY Father, hear our prayers for those who have died; that those now being purified may speedily be brought to your heavenly kingdom, and we pray that we who are now left here on earth may take courage; with faith that is stronger, with hope that is firmer, and charity that is ever unfailing. Through Jesus Christ our Lord, who lives and reigns with you in the unity of the Holy Spirit, one God for ever and ever. Amen.

A hymn may now be sung. Meanwhile, individual candles are lit from the paschal candle, and may then be taken for placing on the graves of loved ones. The people are invited to stand beside these graves. Those remembering people buried elsewhere could be invited to stand somewhere else significant: by a cemetery cross or crucifix, for example, and place their candles there. The priest then should walk along each row of graves, sprinkling them with holy water, and praying a little with each family, group or individual he encounters at a graveside, enquiring, if necessary, who is buried there. He could use a prayer such as the following.

ALMIGHTY God, who see the fall of the sparrow and have counted every hair on our heads, we pray your fatherly care and protection for (N. and N. / those) who rest in this grave, awaiting the resurrection. May they speedily be brought to a place of light and peace, and so come one day to experience the fullness of the salvation Christ won for us, who lives and reigns with you and the Holy Spirit, one God for ever and ever. Amen.

May Almighty God bless this grave, and grant rest to all whose bodies sleep here in the hope of resurrection: Father, Son ✠ and Holy Spirit. Amen.

or

ALMIGHTY God, who by the descent of your only-begotten Son into the tomb have sanctified the grave as a bed of rest for your holy people, we ask you again to bless ✠ this grave, and send your holy angel from heaven to guard it until the day of resurrection dawns, and we all arise to look on you in our flesh. Through the same Christ our Lord. Amen.

FOR THOSE WHO ARE REMEMBERING LOVED ONES BURIED ELSEWHERE

ALMIGHTY God, kindest comforter of those who mourn, hear our prayers for those buried far away. Be comfort in our sorrow, and grant rest to those we love who have died, we pray, and be with all your faithful children until the day of resurrection dawns, and we shall for ever be united with you in heaven. Through Christ our Lord. Amen.

FOR PARENTS AT THE GRAVE OF THEIR CHILD

HEAVENLY Father, we commit this child into your loving care. We confidently call you Father, for our earthly parenthood is only a reflection of your own eternal goodness towards those called your children. So confidently we entrust N. to your loving care, thanking you for lending him/her to us a little while, and looking forward to that day when our earthly family will, in your grace, be re-united, in Christ Jesus our Lord. Amen.

May Almighty God bless this grave, and all whose bodies sleep here in the hope of resurrection: Father, Son ✠ and Holy Spirit. Amen.

It would be a good idea to conclude this service on a positive note; if a church is nearby, one might celebrate Benediction of the Blessed Sacrament. Otherwise a simple Our Father and blessing will have to suffice. A warm drink and some comforting conversation would probably be a good idea.

ST CECILIA'S DAY

BLESSING OF A CHOIR

The choir should sing something appropriate, commensurate with their ability.

Let us pray.

HEAVENLY Father, we praise you for the gift of music, sent to lighten our lives and lift our hearts to you. We pray for those who assist at our worship by the exercise of musical talent, that they may do so with full hearts, singing not just with the voice but with understanding also, that they may come one day to join the celestial choir in whose worship they participate on earth.

And so, heavenly Father, we ask you, through the intercession of St Cecilia, to inspire and bless our choir in the name of the Father, and of the Son, ✠ and of the Holy Spirit. Amen.

INDEX

CPSIA information can be obtained
at www.ICGtesting.com
Printed in the USA
BVHW011953121221
623862BV00002B/51